This provocative book challenges an understanding of Paul on women's ministry that many have long thought to be beyond question. But historical cross-examination confirms Dickson's case in a way that makes appropriate a rethinking of practice.

J. I. PACKER, Board of Governors' Professor of Theology, Regent College

Can anything new possibly be said in the endless debates over gender roles in the church? If something new is said, could it possibly be true? The answers to both questions are "yes"! John Dickson has recognized the limited, technical sense of "teaching" in many ancient religious contexts, including Christian ones, especially Paul, and consistently in the Pastoral Epistles. Applying this recognition to 1 Timothy 2:12, he has convincingly demonstrated that even a conservative complementarian has no exegetically based grounds for preventing women from delivering sermons. He wisely bypasses entirely larger questions of ordination and leadership for this one virtually incontrovertible observation. That many complementarians continue to controvert it demonstrates the extent to which, however unwittingly, they are bound to the "traditions of men" rather than to the Word of God!

CRAIG L. BLOMBERG, Distinguished Professor of New Testament,
Denver Seminary

Paul, of course, has women "praying" and "prophesying" in the meeting. So, why not also "teaching"? Must one downplay or discard this ban? In this book, however, we learn that we have been missing the special force of that word anyway. With John Dickson, a careful researcher into the context and setting of the New Testament, we uncover its history. This is no mere "battle over words." Apart from instinct and the bare data, all meaningful knowledge (i.e., "science") is revealed through enquiry (i.e., "history"). The testimony of this gifted expositor convincingly discloses the lost meaning of Paul's "teaching."

EDWIN JUDGE, Emeritus Professor of History, Macquarie University

T0045811

A compelling argument grounded in careful exegesis and evidencing a robust view of biblical authority. Those who already agree with Dickson's conclusions and those who don't have much to learn here. I know I did.

GRAHAM COLE, Anglican Professor of Divinity,
Beeson Divinity School, Samford University

Some of us say we give supreme authority to the Bible, and yet we can be pretty confused (at best) or careless (at worst) in how we use biblical words. Was there any difference in the NT between preaching, teaching, exhorting, prophesying, evangelizing, etc? I confess I had never given the matter much thought, being content to know they were all among the rich gifts of God's Spirit for the blessing of his whole church. But John Dickson's detailed survey and careful distinctions should make us all think again. Whatever our view on what kinds of ministry women should or should not exercise, and whether or not we are convinced by the author's conclusions (as I am), this book forces us to bring our thinking and our practice to Scripture and test them there.

DR. CHRIS WRIGHT, International Ministries Director, Langham Partnership

Revised Edition

# Hearing
# Her Voice

The author has waived all royalties and income from this book.

Fresh Perspectives on Women in Ministry

**Revised Edition**

# Hearing Her Voice

## A Case for Women Giving Sermons

## John Dickson

 ZONDERVAN®

ZONDERVAN

*Hearing Her Voice, Revised Edition*
Copyright © 2012, 2014 by John Dickson

This title is available as a Zondervan ebook.
Visit www.zondervan.com/ebooks.

Requests for information should be addressed to:

Zondervan, 3900 Sparks Drive SE, Grand Rapids, Michigan 49546

ISBN 978-0-310-51927-0

Cover design: Ron Huizinga
Interior design and composition: Greg Johnson, Textbook Perfect

Printed in the United States

HB 11.17.2023

For Sophie and Josephine

# Contents

## Abbreviations

| | |
|---|---|
| ICC | International Critical Commentary |
| JETS | *Journal of the Evangelical Theological Society* |
| JSNT | *Journal for the Study of the New Testament* |
| JTS | *Journal of Theological Studies* |
| NIGTC | New International Greek Testament Commentary |
| NIBC | New International Biblical Commentary |
| TSAJ | Texte und Studien zum antiken Judentum |
| WBC | Word Biblical Commentary |
| WUNT | Wissenschaftliche Untersuchungen zum Neuen Testament |

## Introduction

# A Very Modest Argument

> Let a woman learn quietly with all submissiveness. I do not permit a woman to teach or to exercise authority over a man; rather, she is to remain quiet. (1 Timothy 2:11–12)

The question of women delivering sermons in church is a touchy one for many evangelical Christians. For some it is even a test case of whether someone *is* an evangelical. I remember the dismay of one of my pastor friends when he was told by his ecclesiastical superior, "It is sinful for a woman to preach, and sinful for a man to let her." Such language powerfully raises the stakes. We want to get this issue right.

Strong feelings about women delivering sermons arise mainly because the Bible is interpreted to forbid a woman to preach (1 Tim. 2:12). In part, it is also because inviting women into the pulpit is seen as a first step on a slippery slope to women holding the full range of offices in the church. This short book has nothing to say about ecclesiastical offices. Rather, it is about whether it is biblical to invite women to give the twenty- to thirty-minute message in the church service. Having long believed otherwise, I now think the answer is *yes*.

My argument is straightforward (even if it takes a while to provide a full account and to answer potential objections). Put simply, there are numerous public-speaking ministries mentioned in the New Testament—teaching, exhorting, evangelising, prophesying, reading, and so on—and Paul restricts *just one of them* to qualified males: "teaching." Given that he repeatedly describes these various functions as "different," it is essential to know what the apostle means by "teaching" and whether the modern sermon is its true counterpart. If today's sermons more closely resemble what Paul called "exhortation," for instance, that would surely change the relevance of 1 Timothy 2:12 for the discussion, since that passage has nothing to say about exhortation.

The word "sermon" is not a biblical term. It comes from the Latin *sermo*, or "discourse, talk." But "sermon" and "teaching" have become virtually synonymous. When a church today is described as having "good teaching," most evangelicals presume the reference is to "good sermons." Thus the thrust of Paul's injunction, "I do not permit a woman to teach," seems clear: women must not deliver sermons. This is what we might call the "plain sense" reading. Rarely do we consider whether this reading assumes *our* use of the term "teaching" rather than Paul's.

I hope to show that the specific activity Paul disallows women in 1 Timothy 2:12 does not refer to a general type of speaking based on Scripture. Rather, it refers to a specific activity found throughout the pages of the New Testament, namely *preserving and laying down the traditions handed on by the apostles*. This activity is different from the explanation and application of a Bible passage found in today's typical expository sermon. I don't dispute that *some* sermons continue to function as "teaching" in Paul's sense, but I struggle to believe that most (or even many) do. If this is correct—if Paul's "teaching" and our "sermon" are not always identical—the biblical warrant for excluding women from the pulpit is questionable.

Let me offer an imperfect analogy. Imagine that 1 Timothy 2:12 actually read, "I do not permit a woman to *prophesy* to a man." I doubt we would take this to mean that *all* forms of public speaking in church were forbidden to women. We would work hard to understand exactly what Paul meant by "prophesying" and then avoid asking women to give that kind of message. The *specificity* of the word "prophesying," then, would prevent us from applying this command to all speaking ministries. Let me be clear: I do not intend to argue, as some have done, that "prophesying" and sermons are identical. I offer this as an analogy. My point is that we have universalised the word "teaching" as though it refers to all kinds of Bible-based talks in church, when in Paul's usage, "teaching" is *at least* as specialised as "prophesying" (probably more so).

On a personal note, I was led to the Christian faith by a woman—a woman *preacher*. However, once I came across 1 Timothy 2:12, I felt uncomfortable that my "mother" in the faith seemed to disregard, or explain away, what seemed to me to be the clear ruling of Paul ("I do not permit a woman to teach"). It wasn't until about ten years into my ministry as a singer, preacher, and evangelist that I began to doubt that 1 Timothy 2:12 referred to "sermons" specifically. It took several more years to feel comfortable asking out loud the questions raised here.

I should make clear at the start that I am not arguing—directly or indirectly—for women's ordination to the priesthood or as senior pastors. I am only making the case that trained and godly women should be allowed to give sermons. For many, then, this book will be disappointingly un-revolutionary, a betrayal of the egalitarian spirit that flows from the gospel. I am conscious that in many parts of the evangelical world—in the UK, US, China, Africa, and my native Australia—it will seem quaint, if not bizarre, that so much effort would be spent on urging churches to let women deliver sermons. Equally, those on the other side of this debate may see what follows as a stealthy nod toward women's ordination and therefore as evidence of my acquiescing to the spirit of the age. Such readers should take note of the modest scope of my position: women should be allowed to give sermons.

I have often thought it would be much easier to endorse one complete package or the other, to be a full-blown "complementarian" or a card-carrying "egalitarian" (labels I dislike).[1] There is certainly more "tribal support" found in doing so. Rarely is the midway position between two hotly contested sides the path of convenience. Nevertheless, I am compelled and constrained by what I think God's Word teaches—as are my detractors on either side.

My goal in what follows is to explain why I now think I was mistaken to stand against women giving sermons. I want to invite my friends and colleagues to reassess (again) the biblical basis of their own reticence to invite women into the pulpit. I do not imagine I will change many minds; such is the strength of theological conviction and camaraderie around this issue. I do hope, however, that I can demonstrate that it is possible to operate with a thoroughly conservative evangelical theology and methodology, employing no "liberal fancy footwork," and to arrive at the conclusion that women should be able to explain and apply the Bible in the power of the Spirit for the building up of the whole congregation.

This is not an academic book. I hope it displays the thoughtfulness and care of a piece of scholarship, but it is really only intended as a thoughtful conversation starter for ministers, lay workers, small group leaders, and other interested evangelicals. Unlike some of my other books, I have decided not to pepper the argument with interesting stories, illustrations, and examples. What the book lacks in "colour," however, I hope it makes up for in brevity. I want readers to understand my argument and to move onto their own reflections about how, or whether, any of my thinking should impact their particular situation. The questions at the end are grouped around the four chapters (and conclusion) and can be used for guided discussion and criticism within staff teams and small group Bible studies. I have tried to prepare questions that give as much scope to disagreeing with the book as agreeing with it.

Finally, I need to make clear that my argument is not in any way intended to devalue the terrific things women are already doing in my own conservative evangelical circles. I would hate my emphasis on sermons to suggest that eternally valuable ministry is not taking place out of the pulpit: as women lead small groups, inspire people to reach out, conduct care services, follow up newcomers, read the Bible one-on-one with other women, preach to other women, and so on. My point is not that women should be able to do the "real" work of preaching to mixed congregations—still less that there should be "symmetry" between the sexes in church. Rather, I hope to explain why I think we have been unnecessarily cautious in excluding women from giving sermons.

# Part 1

# Teaching Isn't Everything:
# What 1 Timothy 2:11–12 Cannot Mean

**In a nutshell:** There are numerous speaking ministries mentioned in the Bible: teaching, exhorting, prophesying, evangelising, reading, and so on. They are clearly "different" activities. The apostle Paul certainly forbids women to "teach," but he nowhere asks them not to engage in other forms of public speaking.

Let me start with what our key text cannot mean. Most agree that 1 Timothy 2:11–12 is not forbidding women to speak God's truth to men in *all* circumstances. That interpretation would bring the passage into conflict with other texts that happily envisage various speaking roles for women.

## 1.1. Women Speaking in the New Testament

Paul tells the Corinthians that "every [woman] who *prays* or *prophesies* with her head uncovered dishonors her head" (1 Cor. 11:5, italics added). The remark obviously concerns activities in the public church service, as most commentators agree.[2] Paul is therefore happy for women to *prophesy* to men.

In Acts 21:9 we likewise hear about the four daughters of Philip the evangelist "who prophesied." The description (stated in the Greek present tense) suggests that this was the well-known and ongoing function of these women in the church of Caesarea. What Paul describes in 1 Corinthians 11:5 and what Luke details in Acts 21:9 are no doubt the fulfillment of Joel 2:28, quoted on the day of Pentecost by the apostle Peter in Acts 2:17: "your sons *and your daughters* shall prophesy" (italics added).

If we equated sermons (even just *some* sermons) with prophesying, there would be no need for further argument: women were giving sermons in the New Testament. This is not my argument, but it does highlight the need to understand what the various New Testament speaking activities involved before deciding what women are and aren't allowed to do. The strict identification of the modern "sermon" with what Paul calls "teaching" can be questioned.

Women may also clarify the true content of the gospel to a man. In Acts 18:26 we read, "[Apollos] began to speak boldly in the synagogue, but when Priscilla and Aquila heard him, they took him aside and explained to him the way of God more accurately." This is not *public* teaching, but it is equally clear that Priscilla did not play "second fiddle" in this crucial ministry of theological correction. She is named first (as she is also in Rom. 16:3, where Paul calls her a "fellow worker," a term usually reserved for fellow missionaries), and the verb form is in the plural ("they . . . explained"). This surely means Priscilla was *as active as* her husband in conveying the truth of Christ to Apollos.

Please don't misunderstand my point. I am not offering a "balancing" argument, as if Paul's restriction in 1 Timothy 2:11–12 must be *held in tension* with the fact that, elsewhere in the Bible, women may speak God's Word to men. I am simply highlighting that there are different types of speaking roles mentioned in the New Testament (prophesying, explaining, teaching) and only one of them is restricted to men.

Women probably also served as fellow workers in Paul's evangelistic preaching. In passing, the apostle speaks of "women [Euodia and Syntyche], who have labored side by side with me in the gospel together with Clement and the rest of my fellow workers" (Phil. 4:3).

The language used here suggests personal involvement in proclaiming the gospel, not just some ancillary mission activity like showing hospitality or giving money, since the expression "in the gospel" is often interpreted by New Testament specialists as shorthand for "in the task of preaching the gospel."[3] These women were probably key evangelists in the founding of the church at Philippi.

"Evangelism" is not the same as "teaching," of course, but that is part of the point I want to make. There are *different* types of proclamation in the New Testament, and only one of them is "not permitted" to women.

## 1.2. Women Speaking in the Old Testament

Not without relevance are the Old Testament examples of female leadership and/or speaking among God's people. The prophet Miriam led a chorus of women in singing a prophetic message to all Israel in Exodus 15:20–21, and in Micah 6:4 she is recalled as having been "sent before" Israel, a clear description of her leadership (alongside Moses and Aaron). Deborah in Judges 4–5 is both a prophet and a warrior, and, as with Miriam, part of her message was delivered through song. Then there is Huldah in 2 Kings 22:14–20 and 2 Chronicles 34:22–28, a particularly curious example of spiritual leadership. Not only did she deliver an authoritative message to King Josiah concerning all Judah, but she also validated the authority of the newly rediscovered "Book of the Law of the Lord" (2 Chron. 34:14). One contemporary scholar has remarked that Huldah's endorsement of the document "stands as the first recognizable act in the long process of canon formation."[4]

The ministry of these women should not be dismissed as strange exceptions to the rule of female noninvolvement in the building up of God's people any more than 1 Timothy 2:11–12 should be treated as an exception that applied to the unusual circumstances of

Timothy's ministry in Ephesus (as many argue).[5] Both belong to the biblical data that has to be considered when trying to understand where and how women may be involved in the church.

To repeat what I said earlier, my argument is not that such examples counterbalance what Paul says in 1 Timothy 2:11–12. Not for a moment am I imagining that the prophetic work of Huldah, for example, is the equivalent of New Testament "teaching" and so must be held in tension. I am simply observing that whereas the authority to *teach* the church is restricted to men in the Bible, other significant roles involving speech and leadership are not.

A couple of related questions surface at this point. First, since women can engage in *several* forms of speaking God's Word, what specific activity does Paul withhold from them in 1 Timothy 2:12? Second, is there any basis on which we can equate this activity with a modern sermon? In other words, how does "teaching" differ from the other speaking activities in New Testament church life, and why is the modern "sermon" always thought to fulfill that function? These are the important issues I plan to explore in the following sections.

## 1.3. Prophesying and Teaching

The specific Greek word used in 1 Timothy 2:12 is *didaskō*. We translate it "to teach," but of course, that does not mean Paul used the term to refer to everything we today might call teaching. In the English language, "teach" has broad connotations. In Christian circles it may refer to any sort of biblical talk. As a result, some evangelicals balk at allowing women to facilitate Bible study groups, give book reviews, or even lead or "emcee" a church service.

There are excellent reasons for thinking that Paul did not regard *didaskō* as a "catch-all" term. In fact, he seems to have thought of it as a specific activity, easily distinguishable from other types of speech mentioned in his letters, such as praying, prophesying, speaking in tongues, evangelising, reading (Scripture), exhorting, and admonishing. Obviously, all of these activities are related since they all convey God's truth to others but the overlap does not dissolve the distinctions. Let me unpack this a little.

In 1 Corinthians 12:28 a distinction is made between prophets and teachers:

> And God has appointed in the church first apostles, second prophets [*prophētēs*], third teachers [*didaskalos*], then miracles, then gifts of healing, helping, administrating, and various kinds of tongues.

The activity of teachers and the activity of prophets cannot be the same. Paul's use of "first," "second," and "third" makes that clear. Whatever overlap there may be in the content and function of prophets and teachers, that overlap does not negate the distinction between them.

Twice in 1 Corinthians 14, Paul distinguishes "teaching" from other types of speech that might occur in a congregational setting: "How will I benefit you unless I bring you some revelation or knowledge or prophecy or teaching [*didachē*]?" (14:6). The fact that Paul allows women to "prophesy" (1 Cor. 11:5) but not to "teach" (1 Tim. 2:12) is proof enough that he thought of these activities as distinct. Again, a few paragraphs later he writes, "When you come together, each one has a hymn, a lesson [teaching; *didachē*], a revelation, a tongue, or an interpretation" (1 Cor. 14:26). Obviously, Paul sees "teaching" as a *particular* activity, distinguishable in some way from other types of public speaking one would expect to hear regularly in the church service.

Especially interesting is the fact that throughout the discussion of Christian gatherings in 1 Corinthians 12–14, "teaching" has little prominence; it is "prophesying" that gets most of the attention (14:1, 3, 5, 22, 24–25, 29–32). As we have already seen, prophesying is open to women. This fact alone raises a significant question mark over any reticence we may have to invite women to speak in church. In our intended faithfulness to the specific prohibition of 1 Timothy 2:12, we are in danger of being unfaithful to the equally clear expectations of 1 Corinthians 14.

But what is prophesying? Some insist that, while we know what "teaching" is (exposition of Scripture, it is thought), we do not know what Paul means by "prophesying," so it is best left to one side. For some this may be an avoidance strategy: *Sure, Paul lets women prophesy, but since we don't know what that involved, we needn't worry about its modern application!*

Others avoid discussions about prophesying because of its "spooky" connotations. In evangelical circles, too much has been made of the supposedly *impromptu* and *Spirit-led* character of prophecy, as if these two qualities are what distinguish the activity from preaching, teaching, exhorting, and so on. The emphasis on these twin characteristics of "prophecy" in charismatic circles today makes those of us who worry about such excesses all the more nervous about even discussing contemporary analogies to prophecy. But perhaps our charismatic friends have simply done with prophecy what evangelicals have done with "teaching." They have appropriated the biblical word for their own church experience, and this in turn defines its usage for everyone in the group.

Whatever the case, it should be noted that most of the public speaking referred to in the book of Acts, for instance, would have to be described as impromptu and Spirit-led, whether speeches in the synagogue, in the marketplace, on trial, or in Christian gatherings. The notion of a carefully prepared exposition of Scripture, which we have equated with "teaching," is virtually absent from Acts (as I will discuss in chapter 3).

What is distinctive about prophecy, then, if not its impromptu and Spirit-led character? In 1 Corinthians 12–14 prophesying is marked out by its clarity (in contrast to tongues) and its purpose. That purpose is described plainly by Paul in 1 Corinthians 14:1–3:

> Pursue love, and earnestly desire the spiritual gifts, especially that you may prophesy. For one who speaks in a tongue speaks not to men but to God; for no one understands him, but he utters mysteries in the Spirit. On the other hand, *the one who prophesies speaks to people for their upbuilding and encouragement and consolation.* (italics added)

This is as close to a definition of prophecy as we will find in the New Testament. Paul says it is *comprehensible speech that builds, encourages, and/or consoles* members of the church. This is not far off what preachers might want to say about the purpose of their own sermons. In his important commentary on 1 Corinthians, Anthony Thiselton insists that prophesying is "the public proclamation of gospel truth as applied pastorally and contextually to the hearers," and it "may include applied theological teaching, encouragement, and exhortation to build the church, not merely (if at all) . . . 'spontaneous' mini-messages."[6]

I am not saying that sermons *are* prophecy, as other evangelicals have suggested,[7] only that there are some essential similarities between them that are often overlooked in favour of viewing sermons only ever as "teaching." This does not have a strong biblical basis. Personally, I think the closest New Testament term for what we do in sermons—explaining and applying the Bible in the power of the Spirit—is "exhorting" (discussed below), but in the end, there may not be a precise equivalent. What I am quite sure of, however, is that sermons are *at least* as different from what Paul called "teaching" as they are from what he called "prophesying."

In passing, I want to note that in my own Reformed Anglican tradition, sermons were once called "prophesying." William Perkins (1558–1602), an important Anglican leader of the Puritan movement, wrote *The Art of Prophesying*, an early text on giving sermons. The book is still in print. When Puritans gathered in Elizabethan England and preached to one another, the conferences were apparently called "prophesyings." Personally, I think "exhorting" is a better biblical word for what we do in sermons, but "prophesying" isn't bad. This observation at least underlines that sermons have not been viewed in exactly the same way throughout all of church history.

## 1.4. Exhorting and Teaching

In Romans 12:4–8 Paul refers to three types of speaking— prophesying, teaching, and exhorting. The crucial thing to note is that he goes out of his way to say that these three activities are *not the same*:

> For as in one body we have many members, and the members *do not all have the same function*, so we, though many, are one body in Christ, and individually members one of another. Having gifts that *differ* according to the grace given to us, let us use them: if prophecy [*prophēteia*], in proportion to our faith; if service, in our serving; the one who teaches [*didaskō*], in his teaching [*didaskalia*]; the one who exhorts [*parakaleō*], in his exhortation [*paraklēsis*]; the one who contributes, in generosity; the one who leads, with zeal; the one who does acts of mercy, with cheerfulness. (italics added)

Notice that Paul says these activities "differ" (*diaphoros*) from one another (12:6). The *content* of these three types of speaking may be similar—presumably, they all convey God's truth—but their "function" (*praxis*) is not the same (12:4). We cannot collapse "prophesying" and "exhorting" into "teaching" any more than we can collapse "leading" and "contributing" into "acts of mercy." Otherwise, Paul's metaphor of the body breaks down. This observation is important as we ponder the apostle's meaning in 1 Timothy 2:12. He restricts "teaching" (*didaskō*) to certain qualified men, but he says nothing about "prophesying" or "exhorting."

Again, I am not suggesting that these three forms of speech (teaching, prophesying, and exhorting) are strictly separate or that there is no significant overlap of content and function. I am simply pointing out that, however closely these activities are related, Paul indicates they are *different*.

To recall the analogy I used earlier, imagine if 1 Timothy 2:12 read, "I do not permit a woman to *exhort* a man." I doubt we would think that this meant women could not participate in any public speaking in church, especially when Paul says in Romans 12:6–8 that "exhorting" is not the same thing as "teaching" or "prophesying." Instead, we would try to figure out how exhorting differed from other types of speaking, and then we would make sure we did not ask women to engage in that particular form of discourse. That is what we should be doing with teaching. Instead of giving the term the broadest possible meaning and excluding women from offering any extended speech in church, we should be exploring how teaching differs from prophesying and exhorting and then, from that conclusion, shape our contemporary practice.

We have tended to equate the modern sermon with ancient "teaching." But on what grounds? Why aren't sermons just as appropriately thought of as "exhortation," mentioned in Romans 12:8? This is a form of speech Paul himself is said to have delivered in the synagogue of Pisidian Antioch: "After the reading from the Law and the Prophets, the rulers of the synagogue sent a message to them, saying, 'Brothers, if you have any *word of encouragement* [*logos paraklēseōs*] for the people, say it'" (Acts 13:15, italics added). In this passage, a "word of exhortation" seems to be a public speech following a Scripture reading—not unlike a modern sermon.

Acts 15 provides another example of a "word of exhortation" following a reading. Here, though, it is a new covenant reading. The apostles write a letter to the Gentile churches outlining their decision concerning circumcision and food laws. Two men, Judas and Silas, are sent out with the letter. Their role is to read out the apostolic letter and then to speak to believers about it. The word used for that speaking is "exhorting": "And when they had read it, they rejoiced because of its encouragement [*paraklēsei*]. And Judas and Silas, who were themselves prophets, *encouraged* [*parekalesan*] and strengthened the brothers *with many words* [*dia logou pollou*]" (Acts 15:31–32).

Imagine if Acts 13:15 and 15:31–32 used the term "to teach" for the spoken reflection that followed the reading of the Old Testament and apostolic letter respectively. I suspect these passages would then be offered as evidence that "teaching" and sermons are the same. But I cannot find any New Testament text that employs "to teach" in this way. "Exhortation" seems to be the more apt term.

The same idea is found in the book of Hebrews. So far as I can tell, the closest example in the Bible to a real exposition of biblical passages is found in the extended reflection, explanation, and Christological application of Old Testament texts in this wonderful New Testament book. The author doesn't just offer "proof texts"; he cites passages, makes observations about them, and then discusses their meaning for Christians. The most sustained examples of this are his treatment of Psalm 95 in Hebrews 3–4 and of Jeremiah 31 in Hebrews 8–10, but the whole letter is structured around biblical quotations and reflections. Even if it isn't exposition in the manner taught in preaching classes in evangelical colleges and seminaries today, it is close. My point, however, is that at the end of the book the author provides his own label for what he's been doing throughout. He pleads, "bear with my *word of exhortation*, for I have written to you briefly" (Heb. 13:22, italics added). The expression "word of exhortation" (*logos paraklēseōs*) is identical to that used in Acts 13:15 and similar to that in Acts 15:32. If the Bible has an expression appropriate to describe what we do in the modern expository sermon, it is the "word of exhortation," not "teaching."

In light of Acts 13:15; 15:31–32; and Hebrews 13:22, Paul's comment to his apprentice Timothy in 1 Timothy 4:13 may provide confirmation that a speech following an authoritative reading is "the exhortation." The apostle writes, "Until I come, devote yourself to the public reading of Scripture, to exhortation, to teaching." First, we should note that Paul is referring to three distinct activities. He uses the definite article ("the") in the Greek text before each item. The text says literally, "Devote yourself to *the* reading, to *the* exhortation, to *the* teaching." Scholarship suggests that these ministries are three distinct, well-known functions in Timothy's congregations.[8] In other words, "exhorting" cannot be equated with "teaching" just as neither activity can be equated with "reading."

Second, notice that it is "the exhortation," not "the teaching," that is mentioned immediately after the reference to "the reading." We already know that Paul sees "the one who exhorts" and "the one who teaches" as different functionaries (Rom. 12:6–8). Then, if one of these two activities comes close to a modern sermon—a speech on a Bible reading—it is likely to be "the exhortation." Imagine if the sequence of Paul's words had been "the reading," "the teaching," and then "the exhortation." I am sure that those who understand sermons as teaching would use 1 Timothy 4:13 as evidence for the identification.

"Teaching" does have a strong connection with Scripture, as I will explain in chapter 2, but it cannot be defined as an explanation and application of Scripture. The better term for that expository activity, even if it is not a precise equivalent, is "the exhortation." As I. Howard Marshall observes in his analysis of 1 Timothy 4:13, "The reading of Scripture forms the basis of the second item, the 'exhortation' or sermon." He then defines exhortation as "the exposition of Scripture . . . leading to commands or encouragements."[9]

To be clear, none of this means that all of the New Testament's uses of the word "exhortation" (*paraklēsis*) refer to this formal activity. Often the word means no more than "encouragement," but when the word appears in expressions such as "a word of exhortation" or "the one who exhorts" or "the exhortation," it appears to mark out a distinct activity: *a speech designed to persuade or inspire the congregation on the basis of an authoritative tradition or text.*

## 1.5. A Preliminary Conclusion

My preliminary conclusion is simple. Only *one* of the numerous types of public speaking in church is restricted to men in the New Testament—the activity of "teaching." On what grounds, then, have we made this activity wholly equivalent to the modern sermon, even to the neglect of other forms of New Testament speaking? Why are sermons always considered a form of "teaching," when one might just as easily (*more* easily, in my view) equate them with what Paul calls "the exhortation"?

If I invite my Women's Pastor to stand up after the Bible reading and in the power of the Spirit *exhort* my congregation for twenty minutes to heed and apply God's Word, how does this breach Paul's instructions in 1 Timothy 2:12? She has given a "word of exhortation." Paul only forbids her to "teach." They are not the same thing. I will develop these ideas further, but I want to indicate at this point that this is the heart of my argument. If sermons were exclusively "teaching," I would have no problem excluding women from the pulpit. (That is precisely what I believed for the first decade of my ministry.) However, if sermons—even just *some* sermons—are closer to "exhortation" than they are to "teaching," then what biblical grounds remain for excluding women entirely from this ministry?

In the following chapter I will try to answer the obvious next question: What exactly is "teaching"? Here at the midway point, however, I want to suggest that my preliminary conclusion stands whether or not one accepts my particular—some might think "reductionist"—understanding of "teaching." There are several biblical activities, other than "teaching," that look *somewhat analogous* to what we call a sermon, where an individual speaks to the congregation to nourish Christian faith. All of these other activities are open to women. I believe our churches would be enriched by hearing qualified women deliver such "speeches," whatever we choose to call them.

## Part 2

# Laying It Down: What Teaching Really Is

**In a nutshell:** For Paul, "teaching" (in the technical sense) involved carefully preserving and laying down for the congregation the traditions handed on by the apostles. In the period before the texts of the New Testament were readily available (before about AD 100), a church's only access to the range of things the apostles had said about Jesus and his demands was through a teacher, the one entrusted with the "apostolic deposit."

What is the specific speaking role referred to in 1 Timothy 2:12 as *didaskō*, "to teach"?

## 2.1. General and Technical Teaching

First, we must distinguish between a *general* type of "teaching" and a *specific* or technical meaning of the term. In Colossians 3:16, for example, Paul wants *everyone* in the congregation to be "teaching . . . one another" (*didaskontes . . . heautous*) whenever they are "singing psalms and hymns and spiritual songs." "Teaching" in this sense is a ministry open to all, men and women alike. This meaning of the term is unlike Paul's restrictions to men in 1 Timothy, even if the two types of teaching are closely related.

I have long believed that the songs referred to in Colossians 3:16 were fixed pieces of apostolic hymnic material, similar to what we find in Philippians 2:6–11 and Colossians 1:15–20, and elsewhere. These small examples of the apostolic teaching had been fixed in a manner that allowed everyone to "teach" (i.e., lay down the apostolic traditions) without anyone in particular assuming the authority of the teacher. It is only "teaching authority" that Paul did not permit to women. So when the whole congregation sang apostolically approved hymns, the authority of this "teaching" resided not in an individual preacher but in the fixed words of the song itself.

A more specific or technical use of *didaskō*, "to teach," must be in Paul's mind when he says, "I do not permit a woman to teach or to exercise authority over a man" (1 Tim. 2:12). Here he means a *specific* word-ministry, not a general one performed by the congregation as they sing. It is no doubt the same sort of teaching he mentions in Romans 12:6–8; 1 Corinthians 12:28–29; and 1 Timothy 4:13, where he distinguishes "teaching" from "exhorting," "prophesying," and "reading." The fact that Paul pairs teaching in 1 Timothy 2:12 with "authority" shows that he is thinking of a specific type of teaching, not what goes on when we sing together. As friend and New Testament scholar Claire Smith writes, "teaching" in 1 Timothy 2:12 and throughout the epistle "connotes teaching in a 'technical sense,' not all speech with a didactic element."[10]

"Teaching" in 1 Timothy as a specialised activity, "not all speech with a didactic element," is widely accepted in New Testament scholarship, but let me address more about what scholars mean when they refer to the "technical" use of a word. In all languages, individual terms can serve a variety of purposes. This is because words frequently have root meanings that are broad enough to allow the word to be used in different ways in different contexts. It is not that the word always has the broadest meaning; it is that terms are flexible, sometimes signifying one thing, sometimes signifying another—always related to the root idea.

Consider, for example, the English word "tackle." Suppose you met someone who knew the dictionary definition of the verb "to tackle" (*to make determined efforts to deal with*) but who was completely unacquainted with Rugby Union and its special use of the term. Now imagine you are both at a game and, on seeing a successful Wallabies scrum, your friend declares, "Oh, what excellent tackling!" You would probably want to point out to him that in the context of Rugby the word "tackle" is used with a more specific or technical meaning: *to stop the forward progress of the ball carrier by seizing them and knocking them to the ground.* Your friend's definition is broad enough to be true but not specific enough to be accurate in that context.

"Teaching" in the Bible can be used in a variety of ways. Its root or broad idea is *the transmission of truth from the learned to the learner.* But this does not mean that every instance of the term only has this broad sense, any more than "tackle" only has its root sense. We have to be sensitive to how words are used in their particular context. Otherwise, we are leaving words up the ladder of abstraction, devoid of practical substance. "Teaching" in the Pastoral Epistles (1 and 2 Timothy and Titus), and elsewhere in Paul's letters, usually has a technical or specific sense. It never leaves behind the abstract idea of *transmitting truth* (just as "tackle" in Rugby does not contradict the broad meaning of the word), but it does *focus* on one specific idea: transmitting intact the new covenant words of the apostles.[11]

"Teaching" as *transmitting intact the new covenant words of the apostles* has its closest old covenant equivalent in Moses' famous statement to Israel: "And now, O Israel, listen to the statutes and the rules that I am *teaching* you, and do them, that you may live, and go in and take possession of the land that the LORD, the God of your fathers, is giving you. You shall not add to the word that I command you, nor take from it" (Deut. 4:1–2, italics added). Here Moses delivers the oral tradition of the law. He heard it from God and "taught" it to Israel ("teach" here in Deuteronomy is *lamad* in the Hebrew text and *didaskō* in the Greek text of Paul's day). The nation was to receive this law without adding or taking from it, expressions that emphasize the *fixed* nature of the material. Another reference to "teaching" in Deuteronomy concerns the role of parents:

> You shall therefore lay up these words of mine in your heart and in your soul, and you shall bind them as a sign on your hand, and they shall be as frontlets between your eyes. You shall *teach* them to your children, talking of them when you are sitting in your house, and when you are walking by the way, and when you lie down, and when you rise. You shall write them on the doorposts of your house and on your gates. (Deut. 11:18–20)

In both of these passages it is clear that to "teach" does not mean to *expound* or *explain*; it means to *transmit words intact*. In a new covenant setting this is exactly the authoritative activity Paul restricts to certain men.

Consider again the relationship between the words "teaching" and "authority" in 1 Timothy 2:12, "I do not permit a woman to teach or to exercise authority over a man." Grammatically, Paul could be giving two loosely related instructions: women are not to teach men, nor are they to have authority over men. But the grammar equally supports reading this as one instruction described in two dimensions: women are not to exercise *the authority of teaching*. While the latter makes better sense of Paul's sentence structure, there are important scholars on both sides of the debate. Happily (for many readers), I have relegated my discussion of this finer point to an endnote,[12] since my overall argument fits with either view.

Even if Paul means that a woman can neither teach nor have authority, the authority in question must refer to that of being an "elder" (discussed in Paul's section immediately following: 1 Tim. 3:1–7). Paul cannot mean *any kind of authority at all*, since that would contradict what he says elsewhere. When a woman prophesies in church (1 Cor. 11:5), assuming her prophecy is accepted as conforming to God's truth, she surely has engaged in an authoritative activity, even if that authority derives from the apostolic truth and is subject to the male elders. The same could be said of a woman's sermon. The authority derives from Scripture and is subject to the elders. This is not quite how I draw the threads together, and I am not equating modern sermons with ancient prophecy. I offer this reflection simply to underline that, even if one interprets 1 Timothy 2:12 as referring to the two activities of teaching and exercising authority (of the elder), one could still agree that women may preach some kinds of sermons. With that said, as I have tried to show in endnote 12, "authority to teach" is the more obvious meaning of Paul's words in this text.

So what is "teaching" in this formal, authoritative sense? A good answer to this question should address both historical realities and biblical texts. Let me offer a brief word, then, about the use of history in interpreting Scripture.

## 2.2. The Use of Historical Background to Understand the Bible

Some get nervous about "historical background." They think it can become a form of "secret knowledge" imposed on the text of Scripture to overturn its plain meaning. They are right. History *can* sometimes be used like this, as can Greek grammar and systematic theology. A deep knowledge of Greek grammar and syntax (which, like history, is not an exact science) can be employed to evade or distort the meaning of a passage of the Bible. Such knowledge may also be used to illuminate the meaning of a passage. Modern readers thus find themselves at the mercy of the expert (as they are anyway, since any English translation was produced by specialists in the first place). Systematic theology is similarly hazardous. Theologians, as much as historians and linguists, can force a passage into a doctrinal framework that distorts its meaning significantly. Likewise, theological parameters may elucidate the meaning of a passage.

New Testament specialists ought to have a grasp of all three disciplines: Greek language, first-century history, and systematic theology. Equally, it is crucial that they use these tools *to shed light* on Scripture, *not to distort its meaning*. The lens of history, properly employed, does not obscure the text; instead, it gives us sharper vision to see what is really there—what we perhaps have overlooked because of our existing cultural lenses.

Every Bible reader comes to the text with a set of lenses, whether African Pentecostals, Sydney Anglicans, or American evangelicals. The beauty of knowing biblical history is that it gives you a second pair of lenses, one that can modify your own cultural perceptions and helps you to think a little more like the original recipients of these ancient documents. None of this takes away from the fact, of course, that God's Spirit speaks truly and clearly to us from the pages of Scripture. He does so, however, through what the Westminster Confession calls the "ordinary means."[13] Most of us in Reformed evangelical circles understand "ordinary means" to include *some* knowledge of biblical language, theology, and history. I hope readers will find that the following historical observations, none of which are controversial in scholarship today, will clarify rather than confuse the meaning of 1 Timothy 2:12.

We have already seen that teaching cannot refer to all types of speaking; Paul says it is different from exhorting, prophesying, reading, and so on. Historical and exegetical considerations will make clear that teaching for Paul means *preserving and laying down the fixed traditions of and about Jesus as handed on by the apostles*. Teaching is not explaining a Bible text, nor is it applying God's truth to congregational life (though it can involve both of these things); it is making sure that the apostolic words and rulings are well known and regularly rehearsed in church.

## 2.3. Oral Tradition in Christianity

At the time 1 Timothy was written (early 60s AD), there was no New Testament canon. This requires careful pondering and a little imagination, but it is not in dispute. In the period we are talking about, none of the Gospels had yet been written, and churches had no compendium of apostolic letters. All they had access to were the Old Testament and perhaps one or two Christian documents. The Corinthians, for example, had two or three letters of Paul (written in the mid-to-late 50s), but they did not have the letters Paul wrote a couple years earlier to the Thessalonians 500 km. away. Likewise, the Thessalonians had their own two letters (written around the year 50), but they did not have access to the Corinthian correspondence.

Second Peter 3:15–16 indicates that the recipients of the letter already had at least one letter from Paul (and then another from Peter). It also shows that Peter himself had knowledge of some of Paul's letters. However, in this early period there was no collection of apostolic letters available to the church.

More importantly, scholarship is in wide agreement that the Gospels were all written *after* Paul's letters: Mark in the mid-60s AD, Luke and Matthew in the decade or two following, and John anywhere between the 60s and the 90s. Even the most conservative scholar today would baulk at dating the Gospels before the middle of the 60s, that is, before Paul wrote the Pastoral Epistles.[14] Idiosyncratic arguments can be made to push the writing of the Gospels to an earlier period, but they are simply not plausible (though it would otherwise assist my work of defending the historicity of the Gospels). As any standard introduction to the New Testament will attest—for example, the volume by D. A. Carson and Douglas Moo[15]—date ranges of AD 50–65 for the writing of Paul's epistles and 65–95 for the writing of the Gospels are well-founded and almost universally accepted in contemporary scholarship (with the exception of liberal scholars, who frequently date some of Paul's letters and the Gospels to a later period).

There is another critical additional point. The few letters the Corinthians had received from Paul were not the sum total of what they knew about the new covenant. Let's conduct a thought experiment. Imagine if 1 and 2 Corinthians were all that the Corinthians had learned about the Christian faith. They would know nothing about Jesus' birth, his parables, the Sermon on the Mount, the miracles, the (mis)adventures of the disciples, Jesus' trial, or even any details about his crucifixion, appearances, and command to evangelise the world. They would also have had no "psalms, hymns and spiritual songs" to sing in church (1 Cor. 14:26), since Paul's letters to Corinth contain no hymnic material.

Instead, 1 and 2 Corinthians represent only a tiny proportion of what such a church had received from the apostles concerning Jesus' life, teaching, death and resurrection, and what it means to live by his gospel. The Corinthians were also taught hymns. Proof of what Paul and others had already taught them may be found in the numerous references within the letters already taught the Corinthians (1 Cor. 1:14–17; 2:2; 3:10; 6:9–11; 9:3–6; 11:2, 23–26; 15:1–11). Remember, Paul spent eighteen months teaching the Corinthians *in person* (Acts 18:11), long before he wrote them a letter. We can safely say, on biblical and historical grounds, that 1 and 2 Corinthians probably represent less than 1 percent of the teaching the Corinthians had learned from their apostle.

How, then, were these apostolic teachings about Jesus preserved and protected in the early churches, if not by written documents? The answer is: oral tradition. Christian doctrine in the early decades of the church was maintained, for the most part, not in writings but through the memorizing and rehearsing of the fixed information the apostles had laid down for the churches. We catch glimpses of this process when Paul says things like:

> For I received from the Lord what I also delivered to you, that the Lord Jesus on the night when he was betrayed took bread, and when he had given thanks, he broke it, and said, "This is my body which is for you. Do this in remembrance of me." (1 Cor. 11:23–24)

Here, Paul is reminding the Corinthians *in writing* (around the year AD 55/56) of what he had passed onto them *verbally* five or so years earlier. As we will see, the words "delivering / passing on" and "receiving" (*paradidōmi* and *paralambanō* respectively) are technical jargon in the New Testament for transmitting and accepting traditions handed on by word of mouth. There are numerous other examples (see 1 Cor. 11:2; 15:1–5; Gal. 1:6–9; 1 Thess. 4:1–2).

Historians have long known that ancient Mediterranean societies, particularly the Jews, preserved important traditions by word of mouth ("oral tradition"), but here we find evidence that churches did the same thing. This is not surprising, since all of the first church leaders were Jews. Paul himself had been schooled among the Pharisees, a Jewish group especially well-known for receiving and handing on the traditions of previous rabbis. Epistles like 1 Corinthians were not the principal means of laying down the apostolic traditions; they functioned as *written supplements* to an oral tradition that had already been "delivered to" and "received by" the churches over many years.

The significance of oral tradition for both Judaism and Christianity in this first-century period is widely acknowledged.[16] In a society where only about 15 percent of the population could read, oral tradition was the most effective and trusted means of preserving and disseminating important material. Only when all of the books of the New Testament had been written (by the 90s) and made available as a "collection" (sometime in the second century) did *written* tradition begin.

## 2.4. Oral Tradition among the Pharisees

The first Christians inherited the practice of "passing on" and "receiving" traditions from their Jewish environment. Jewish "teachers" in the period were charged with carefully transmitting the practices, prayers, and rulings of the previous rabbis. Some of these traditions were simple "customs," such as how to wash your hands before a meal. Others mandated ritual or liturgical elements, like the correct time and way to say the Shema (the central creed of Judaism, Deut. 6:4-9). Still other traditions involved recalling important sayings or stories of the great sages of Judaism, some of which are reminiscent of episodes in the Gospels, and which usually had some legal implication. Take the following vignette about Rabbi Hanina ben Dosa, who was a contemporary of the apostle Paul:

> When he would pray for the sick he would say "This one shall live" or "This one shall die." They said to him, "How do you know?" He said to them, "If my prayer is fluent, then I know that it is accepted and the person will live. But if not, I know that it is rejected and the person will die."[17]

The main custodians of these Jewish traditions were the Pharisees. The first-century Jewish historian Josephus, a Pharisee himself, makes this plain, using an important term the New Testament also employs for both Jewish and Christian oral transmission:

> The Pharisees passed on [*paradidōmi*] to the people certain regulations handed down by a succession of fathers and not recorded in the Laws of

Moses, for which reason they are rejected by the Sadducaean group, who hold that only those regulations should be considered valid which were written down, and that those derived from the traditions [*paradoseis*] of the fathers need not be observed. And concerning these matters the two parties came to have controversies and serious differences.[18]

Passing on the oral "traditions of the fathers" not contained in the writings of Moses was "the single most distinctive feature of Pharisaism," writes Joachim Schaper in *The Cambridge History of Judaism*.[19] Furthermore, it was through the synagogues that these traditions gained wide influence, for "the synagogue was a thoroughly Pharisaic institution."[20] Jesus also points to the dominance of the Pharisees in the synagogues: "Woe to you Pharisees! For you love the best seat in the synagogues" (Luke 11:43; see also Matt. 23:2).

The memorised traditions of influential rabbis between about 50 BC and AD 200 were eventually collected (and no doubt modified) in ca. AD 200 in a book known as the Mishnah. The Mishnah's place in Judaism is similar to that of the New Testament in Christianity, as we will see. The opening paragraphs of one section of the Mishnah make clear how ancient Jews thought about this book. Not only is its content on par with the written Torah (or Old Testament), the material was thought to *derive* from Moses himself and was passed on through oral tradition right down to the time of Paul and beyond. The following passage has some strong connections with the New Testament:

Moses received the Law [i.e., the oral Torah] from Sinai and committed it to Joshua, and Joshua to the elders, and the elders to the Prophets; and the Prophets committed it to the men of the Great Synagogue [the time of Ezra]. They said three things: Be deliberate in judgement, raise up many disciples, and make a fence around the Law. Simeon the Just [third century BC] was of the remnants of the Great Synagogue. He used to say: By three things is the world sustained: by the Law, by the Temple service, and by deeds of loving-kindness. Antigonus of Soko received the Law from Simeon the Just. He used to say: Be not like slaves that minister to the master for the sake of receiving a bounty, but be like slaves that minister to the master not for the sake of receiving a bounty; and let the fear of Heaven be upon you. . . . Hillel and Shammai [teachers at the close of the first century BC] received the Law from them. Hillel said: Be of the disciples of Aaron, loving peace and pursuing peace, loving mankind and bring them neigh to the Law. . . . Raban Gamaliel [early first century AD] said: Provide thyself with a teacher and remove thyself from doubt.[21]

While only some Jews today believe that this "oral Torah" truly derives from Moses, few contemporary scholars dispute that the Mishnah is evidence that the rabbis of the first century BC to the second century AD were involved in developing and preserving a vast collection of traditions that were not written down. The concept of two laws—written Scripture and the "traditions of the fathers"—was not formalized until the second century AD, but it was "more or less established by the time of Herod" (i.e., before Jesus), and the oral commandments were "accorded the same legally binding status as Pentateuchal precepts."[22]

Rabbis Hillel and Shammai, mentioned in the Mishnah passage quoted above, were two of the most influential Jewish teachers a generation before Jesus. They founded the two great "schools" of the Pharisees. Scholars often point out the similarity between Hillel's emphasis on "peace" and "love" toward humankind and that found in the teaching of Jesus. What Jesus taught in the synagogues would have resonated with what the custodians of Hillel's oral tradition were also teaching. In other matters, however, the two were poles apart. Hillel, for example, ruled that a man can legitimately divorce his wife if she spoils his dinner. Jesus offered a different perspective.[23]

The Gospels also address Jewish oral tradition, and note that it was the cause of lively debate between the Pharisees and the Lord. Although Jesus accepted the authority of the Old Testament, he publicly denounced many of the ideas taught in Jewish oral tradition. He declared with Isaiah that the Pharisees were "teaching as doctrines [*didaskontes didaskalias*] the commandments of men" (Mark 7:7) and worse, that they were making God's word empty because of their traditions. The passage is worth quoting in full, for it provides New Testament evidence of the prominence of the oral commandments of the Pharisees:

> Now when the Pharisees gathered to him, with some of the scribes who had come from Jerusalem, they saw that some of his disciples ate with hands that were defiled, that is, unwashed. (For the Pharisees and all the Jews do not eat unless they wash their hands properly, holding to the tradition of the elders [*paradosis tōn presbuterōn*], and when they come from the marketplace, they do not eat unless they wash. And there are many other traditions that they observe, such as the washing of cups and pots and copper vessels and dining couches.) And the Pharisees and the scribes asked him, "Why do your disciples not walk according to the tradition of the elders [*paradosis tōn presbuterōn*], but eat with defiled hands?" And he said to them, "Well did Isaiah prophesy of you hypocrites, as it is written,

> "'This people honors me with their lips,
>> *but their heart is far from me;*
>> *in vain do they worship me,*
> teaching as doctrines [*didaskontes didaskalias*] the
>> commandments of men.'

> You leave the commandment of God and hold to the tradition of men" [*paradosis tōn anthrōpōn*]. (Mark 7:1–8)

Jesus then gives an example of teaching based on the Pharisees' repertoire of oral tradition:

> And he said to them, "You have a fine way of rejecting the commandment of God in order to establish your tradition! For Moses said, 'Honor your father and your mother'; and, 'Whoever reviles father or mother must surely die.' But you say, 'If a man tells his father or his mother, "Whatever you would have gained from me is Corban" (that is, given to God)—then you no longer permit him to do anything for his father or mother, thus making void the word of God by your tradition that you have handed down [*paradidōmi*]. And many such things you do. (Mark 7:9–13)

This particular tradition—vowing property to God so that it can't be used by parents—also appears in Mishnah *Nedarim* 5:6. What was sacred lore for the Pharisees was contemptible human teaching for Jesus. Similar criticisms of first-century Jewish oral teachings are found throughout the Gospels (Matt. 16:12; 23:1–22; Mark 1:22; Luke 20:34–40; John 3:10). In all of this, the historical information (from Josephus, the Mishnah, etc.) clarifies Scripture, providing us with clearer lenses to see what was there all along but which, because of our contemporary lenses, we have easily overlooked.

There is an even closer connection between the Mishnah and the New Testament. Gamaliel, listed at the end of the passage quoted above, is the same rabbi mentioned in Acts 5:34 as "a teacher of the law held in honor by all the people." Moreover, Gamaliel's advice in the Mishnah to "provide thyself with a teacher" must have struck a chord with a young Saul (eventually the apostle Paul). This same Gamaliel was Saul's personal teacher in the oral traditions of Judaism. As the apostle himself later tells us in Acts, "I am a Jew, born in Tarsus in Cilicia, but brought up in this city, educated at the feet of Gamaliel according to the strict manner of the law of our fathers, being zealous for God as all of you are this day" (Acts 22:3). This "law of the fathers" isn't a reference to Old Testament law; Paul intends the collection of Pharisaic commandments that Jesus called "traditions of the elders" and Josephus called "traditions of the fathers."

In Galatians 1:14, Paul emphasizes just how seriously he once took these teachings: "And I was advancing in Judaism beyond many of my own age among my people, so extremely zealous was I for the traditions of my fathers." The Greek word for "tradition" in this passage is *paradosis*, the noun related to the verb *paradidōmi* ("pass on"). It is striking that Josephus, Mark, and Paul all use the same vocabulary to describe the oral teachings of the Pharisees. Furthermore, the same terminology is used in the New Testament of the *Christian* oral traditions.

Paul's encounter with Jesus caused him to abandon the Pharisaic "traditions of the fathers." After all, his new teacher and Lord had been profoundly critical of that body of commandments. But Paul didn't forsake the *idea* of oral tradition itself. He embraced a new oral tradition consisting of the stories and teachings of Jesus and the insights the apostles themselves added. "Now I commend you," Paul wrote to the Corinthians, "because you remember me in everything and maintain the traditions [*paradoseis*] even as I delivered them [*paradidōmi*] to you" (1 Cor. 11:2). The Jewish oral tradition Paul had once maintained as a Pharisee had been replaced with a set of Christian oral traditions, which he urged his churches to preserve and obey. Paul also retained from his Jewish background the crucial importance of "teachers." His own Pharisaic teacher, Gamaliel, had emphasized this: "provide thyself with a teacher." The Christian oral tradition, no less than the Jewish oral tradition, required men who could pass on this material with care.

The apostle was the prime teacher in his circle—a new Gamaliel—but he quickly appointed others for the task. He declares to Timothy, "I was appointed a preacher and apostle and teacher"; then he immediately urges him, "Follow the pattern of the sound words that you have heard from me. . . . By the Holy Spirit who dwells within us, guard the good deposit entrusted to you (2 Tim. 1:13–14). A few paragraphs later he insists, "And what you have heard from me in the presence of many witnesses entrust to faithful men who will be able to teach others also" (2:2). Timothy had "heard" Paul's traditions and was now to transmit these to others, who could likewise faithfully pass them on.

Paul's word for this process of preserving and laying down oral tradition is not "exhorting," "prophesying," or "evangelising" but "teaching" (*didaskō*). That's the word used in 1 Timothy 2:12. That's the activity Paul restricts to authorised men. I will say more about this passage later. For now I want to highlight that Paul does not restrict "reading," "exhortation," "prophecy," or "evangelism," but "teaching"—the specific task of preserving and laying down for churches what the apostles had said about Jesus and the new covenant. In all this, Paul's Jewish heritage is clear.

In short, Jesus "handed down" his own authoritative teachings, which for the first Christians replaced the Jewish traditions (of Hillel, Gamaliel, etc.). Jesus called it the gospel of the kingdom (cf. Matt. 4:23; 7:28–29; 9:35). The apostles then became the custodians of this new tradition, adding to it with the authority given to them by the Lord. And they began to pass it on to other reliable men, who could preserve and pass it on to others in a chain of transmission similar to the Jewish tradition described in Josephus and the Mishnah quoted above. These were the "teachers."

## 2.5. The Role of the Teacher before There Was a New Testament

Christian teachers in the period when Paul wrote his letters emulated the Jewish practice of *orally* transmitting important material. They were guardians of a new and different oral tradition from that of the Pharisees. They were charged with memorizing and passing on the teachings of and about Jesus as initially laid down by the apostles.[24] They used Old Testament passages as background and proof for their new covenant message, but exposition of Scripture was not the defining feature of teaching. Instead, teachers were to act as "the congregation's repository of oral tradition," as leading New Testament specialist James Dunn puts it:

We should pause at this point to recall just how crucial teachers were to ancient communities. All who read these pages will have been bred to a society long accustomed to being able to rely on textbooks, encyclopaedias, and other reference works. But an ancient oral society had few if any such resources and had to rely instead on individuals whose role in their community was to function . . . as "a walking reference library."[25]

Consequently, both historical and biblical considerations suggest that "teaching" in 1 Timothy 2:12 refers to *preserving and laying down the body of oral traditions first handed over by the apostles.* This body of traditions was not a collection of documents (yet), and it certainly wasn't a series of expositions through the Old Testament. It was a large collection of memorised sayings and stories of and about Jesus that the apostles passed on, along with their own authoritative rulings and insights on a range of topics.

Numerous references to this set of traditions make clear that although it wasn't written down yet, it was still a body of fixed content. The traditions are variously described as the apostolic "deposit" (1 Tim. 6:20; 2 Tim. 1:14), "the faith that was once for all delivered to the saints" (Jude 3), and the "traditions delivered/received" (1 Cor. 11:2; 15:1–3; 2 Thess. 3:6). Frequently this body of material is called "the teaching" (Rom. 6:17; 16:17; 1 Tim. 1:10; 6:1, 3; Titus 1:9; 2:10; etc.), where it is clear that such teachings do not refer to biblical expositions but recently transmitted apostolic traditions.

Significantly, Paul sometimes places the word "teaching" in synonymous parallelism with "delivered/received." Again, scholars note that "delivered/received" (*paradidōmi/paralambanō*) are Paul's favourite technical terms for the initial laying down of the oral traditions (1 Cor. 11:1; 11:23; 15:3; 1 Thess. 2:13; 4:1; 2 Thess. 3:6). This comes straight from his Jewish heritage, as indicated by his language that describes the "traditions of my fathers" (Gal. 1:14) to which he was formerly devoted as a Pharisee. The word "teaching" appears side by side with this technical vocabulary in Galatians 1:12, where the apostle insists that he came to know the gospel not in the normal human way, as the Galatians did, but through a direct disclosure from Jesus: "I did not *receive* [*paralambanō*] it, nor was I *taught* [*didaskō*] it." For Paul, then, to be "taught" is a perfectly apt alternative term for "receiving" the traditions about Jesus. Similarly, in 2 Thessalonians 2:15 he urges, "So then, brothers, stand firm and hold to the *traditions* [*paradoseis*] that you were *taught* [*didaskō*] by us."

I am not suggesting that "teaching" is an exact synonym for the traditions "delivered/received." The latter almost always refers to the *initial* laying down of apostolic material (which is why it appears in parallel with "evangelising" in 1 Cor. 15:1–3). "Teaching," by contrast, seems to refer to the laying down of the deposit over and over, whether for the first time or the hundredth time. As we will see, in the Pastoral Epistles, written late in Paul's career, the apostle never uses the vocabulary of "delivered/received." "Teaching" stands in its place, consistently referring to the apostolic oral traditions Timothy and Titus were to protect, repeat, and lay down for their churches.[26]

During the apostolic period, there was no written New Testament to read out and expound. Teachers provided Christians with their only record of the apostles' account of Jesus' life and significance. No wonder James the brother of Jesus warned, "Not many of you should become teachers [*didaskaloi*], my brothers, for you know that we who teach will be judged with greater strictness" (James 3:1). To be a repository of the traditions of the apostles was a high calling, for without the ancient teacher there was no access to the material we today can easily read in the Gospels and wider New Testament. Teachers were not simply givers of sermons; they were the primary means of fixing in the minds of churches the foundational deposit first delivered by the apostles.

This basic understanding of "teaching" should not be controversial. In lectures at Moore College years ago, I recall Archbishop Donald Robinson, a careful New Testament specialist, impressing on us the high and sacred duty laid upon teachers: "Teaching is much more specific both as to content and purpose in the NT; it is not just any imparting of information or any sort of discourse. It relates to a specific body of truth, the deposit of the faith."[27] After all, as he also stressed, "at this early stage when the Pauline and other letters were written, the apostle of a church was the single source of both the gospel and the manner-of-life tradition thus articulated for the church."[28]

In other words, there was no authoritative body of texts; there were only authoritative custodians of the tradition. Robinson's lectures prompted my early ponderings that have since resulted in this book. Robinson may not have agreed with me, but I remember wondering at the time in what sense a preacher today could be said to be preserving and laying down that deposit of faith. After all, it is now "deposited" in a set of texts. It resides not in uniquely authorised men, but in the fixed form of the New Testament writings. I can see how an expository sermon *exhorts* people *on the basis* of this apostolic deposit, but no one preserves and lays down this deposit in exactly the way a teacher in the New Testament period was charged. The "sermon" has much in common with "teaching" (as it does with "exhortation"), but the two are not the same.

If there is anything novel in what I am saying, and I suspect there isn't,[29] it is not a particular historical or exegetical insight, still less a new linguistic definition. Again, few New Testament scholars would dispute that before the writing of the New Testament documents, there was a large body of rehearsed oral traditions referred to as "teaching(s)." What I am proposing has to do with the implication and application of these realities. If this is what Paul meant by "teaching," why do we give the same label to a modern sermon? A sermon doesn't usually preserve and lay down the apostolic traditions; it expounds and applies the biblical text in which those traditions are already preserved and laid down. The New Testament activity most closely resembling the task of *speaking after an authoritative reading* is "exhorting" (Acts 13:15; 15:31–32; Heb. 13:22; 1 Tim. 4:13), not "teaching."

An analogy may help illustrate my contention that we have been reading into the word "teaching" a meaning Paul never intended. Imagine discovering a document that declared, "Women are not permitted to play football." Where I come from, this could be read as a reference to four popular sports—Australian Rules (AFL), Rugby League, Rugby Union, and soccer (real football). An Australian, then, could plausibly interpret this ruling as a ban on women playing all football. But what if we knew the document originated in England, where "football" only ever refers to soccer? Suddenly, we would have to conclude that the author of the document only intended to prevent women from participating in one code, not all four. Or if we found that the document was written in a North American context, it would be different again. "Football" could only refer to NFL or what Australians call gridiron. We would then have to conclude that this ban had nothing to say about soccer, AFL, Rugby Union, or Rugby League. The ban was specific to its original setting. It would be inappropriate to extend it to all ball sports involving the foot.

My point is that we tend to read the word "teach" and assume it refers to any extended, biblical speech in church. But Paul's letters come from another time and place. In his usage, "teaching" was not a catchall term for transmitting any Christian truth. It referred to just one type of communication easily distinguishable from "exhorting" and "prophesying." Therefore, 1 Timothy 2:12 is rightly interpreted as prohibiting women to give teaching-sermons, but it cannot be read as a ban on women giving exhorting-sermons (or prophesying-sermons).

Our next step in this discussion is to confront the common opinion that "teaching" for Paul must *also* have included (as a defining characteristic) the exposition of Scripture. After showing that this is not what "teaching" means, I will focus in more detail on Paul's consistent usage of the term in his letters.

# Part 3

# Explain and Apply: How Exposition Differs from Teaching

**In a nutshell:** As vital as biblical exposition is for the life of the church, when Paul refers to "teaching," he never means explaining and applying a Bible passage; rather, he consistently means carefully preserving and laying down for a church what the apostles had said concerning Jesus and his ministry.

Toward the end of this chapter I will explore numerous texts in Paul's letters that confirm the analysis offered so far—that "teaching" means preserving and laying down the fixed traditions of the apostles. Before doing so, however, I want to discuss the practice of *expounding scriptural texts*, which in evangelical circles is equated with "teaching." Our assumption that Paul's word "teaching" and our word "sermon" are identical establishes the so-called "plain sense" reading of 1 Timothy 2:12—women must not give sermons. But once that assumption is questioned, there is nothing plain about that reading. What is not plain to me is that women are not permitted to explain and apply biblical passages (what I consider "exhorting"), but that they are not to preserve and lay down for churches the apostolic traditions concerning Jesus.

## 3.1. Teaching as Scriptural Exposition?

I believe exposition and application of the Bible (in the power of the Spirit) should be the default form of the sermon today, as anyone will discover by listening online to the sermons of my church.[30]

It is a God-honouring response to the reality that we possess his Word in a complete and closed canon of Scripture, in which the apostolic tradition, and much more, is written down. However, the New Testament does equate "teaching" with an "exposition" of a passage of Scripture. With the exception of sections of the book of Hebrews (discussed in ch. 2), exposition as we understand it today hardly features in the New Testament, let alone as the definition of "teaching."[31]

Scholars sometimes argue that several New Testament passages refer to "exposition" and therefore to "teaching." In Acts 8, for example, Philip the evangelist overhears the Ethiopian eunuch reading aloud from Isaiah 53. When the eunuch asks about whom the passage was written, "Philip opened his mouth, and beginning with this Scripture he told him the good news [*euangelizomai*] about Jesus" (Acts 8:35). This is not exposition or teaching. Luke does not say Isaiah 53 *itself* was explained; rather, Philip used this text as a launching pad for his evangelistic presentation of the story of Jesus' life, death, and resurrection—that is, the gospel. The difference is not small.

A second passage interpreted to equate scriptural exposition as teaching is 1 Timothy 4:13: "Until I come, devote yourself to the public reading of Scripture, to exhortation, to teaching." I argued in chapter 1 that Paul is not referring to a single activity: *exhorting people by teaching the Scriptures* (or something similar). The triple use of the definite article—"*the* reading, *the* exhortation, *the* teaching"—suggests three distinguishable, even if related, activities. Elsewhere, as we have also seen, Paul makes clear that exhortation and teaching serve "different" functions (Rom. 12:4–8), even if they can, in the case of Timothy, be performed by one person.

It has been argued that, considering how close "teaching" is to "reading" (i.e., reading the Old Testament Scripture) in 1 Timothy

4:13, teaching denotes the exposition of Scripture. But the order of Paul's words suggests that if any activity has a close connection with Scripture "reading," it must be "exhortation," not "teaching." If that is correct, exhortation would be a Christian reflection on a reading, similar to the "word of exhortation" Paul gave following the Old Testament reading in the synagogue of Pisidian Antioch (Acts 13:15) and the "exhortation" Judas and Silas offered after reading the apostolic letter to Gentile churches (15:31–32). As I have said repeatedly, what we label a sermon is similar to what the New Testament describes as exhortation, an activity nowhere restricted to men.

I am not denying that "teaching" in 1 Timothy 4:13 is *related* to the Old Testament Scriptures. The apostolic traditions often explained how Jesus fulfilled the Law and the Prophets. But this does not make teaching identical with exposition of Scripture. Here Paul is encouraging Timothy to continue doing three important and related public activities: to *read* the Old Testament out loud to the churches, *offer exhortations* designed to warn, correct, console, and so on, and *teach* (i.e., verbally lay down) the apostolic deposit entrusted to him.

Second Timothy 3:16 could also be read as evidence that "teaching" refers to Bible exposition. Paul exhorts Timothy: "All Scripture [again, he means the Old Testament][32] is breathed out by God and profitable for teaching [*didaskalia*], for reproof, for correction, and for training in righteousness, that the man of God may be competent, equipped for every good work."[33] Of course, if we assume that teaching means exposition, this passage yields good evidence, since "teaching" is mentioned immediately after a reference to "Scripture." But two items undermine this. First, in context Paul is not urging Timothy to read Scripture *publicly* and then to teach it publicly. He is telling his apprentice to study the

Scripture *personally* so that he will be better equipped for his public ministry of teaching, rebuking, and the like. In other words, these are not two sequential public activities: reading out the Scripture, then teaching/expounding it. Rather, one is a *preparatory* activity and the other is a *public* one.

Second, Paul says the Scriptures are merely "profitable" (NIV "useful") for Timothy's teaching, not that teaching involves explaining the content of these Scriptures. This is significant. The term *ōphelimos* (translated "profitable/useful") essentially means *beneficial*: studying Scripture is beneficial for Timothy's teaching ministry. This would be an odd way to express the relationship between *Scripture* and *teaching* if Paul believed that teaching *was in fact* the exposition of Scripture. It would be like a soccer coach saying, "Putting the ball in the back of the net is useful for scoring goals." It is not *useful* for scoring goals; it *is* scoring a goal.

There is a better way to understand 2 Timothy 3:16. For Paul, the Old Testament provides a supportive role for the task of laying down the apostolic "teaching." That role is the one I have already mentioned in connection with 1 Timothy 4:13. The apostolic traditions are full of demonstrations that Jesus is the fulfillment of the Law and the Prophets. Studying the Jewish Scriptures, then, is hugely beneficial for Timothy's task of laying down for his churches what the apostles have said (i.e., teaching). But this does not mean that teaching is expounding a Bible passage—as vital as exposition is for the health of the church. Paul, the coach, is saying, "Studying the 'playbook' is useful for scoring goals."

Other arguments could be mounted to show that "teaching" in the New Testament necessarily involves exposition, but none relies on explicit evidence. Rather, they demonstrate that Scripture is related to, or beneficial for, the task of laying down the new covenant message. For example, the Gospels frequently say that Jesus went around "teaching in the synagogues" (e.g., Matt. 4:23; 9:35). Because ancient synagogue services included Scripture readings, what else could Jesus' teaching be, so the argument goes, than an exposition of the Bible reading? The reality is, the Gospels provide many lengthy accounts of Jesus' teaching, and none of them has him expounding Old Testament passages. His teaching frequently *quotes* Scripture as its fulfillment, but it never expounds a text as we expect in a contemporary sermon.

Consider the Sermon on the Mount (Matt. 5–7), Matthew's premier example of the Messiah's "teaching." Allusions to the Old Testament are found throughout, but nowhere does Jesus expound a passage. He merely lays down his own new "law" as the fulfillment of the Law of Moses. Matthew labels the Sermon on the Mount Jesus' "teaching" (*didachē*; 7:28), so we are probably on safe ground in thinking that the Lord offered similar content when he was "*teaching* in the synagogues." A glance through the Gospels' use of the word "teaching" reveals that when it doesn't refer to the traditions of the Pharisees (Matt. 16:12; Mark 7:7), it refers to the new traditions Jesus himself laid down for his disciples (Matt. 5:2; 7:27; Mark 2:13; 4:1–2; 8:31; 9:31; 11:18; 12:38; Luke 4:32; 11:1; John 6:60; 7:16; 8:20). This teaching, *plus* the apostles' remembrances about Jesus, *plus* the apostles' own rulings about the new covenant, eventually form the body of "teaching" found throughout Paul. In any case, it is clear that neither Paul nor Matthew, nor any of the gospel writers, equates teaching with exposition of a biblical text. As central as Scripture was to the teaching of Paul and Jesus, Scriptural exposition is not the defining or constitutive characteristic of their teaching (in the way it is with ours).[34]

The same observations apply to references to the "teaching" of the apostles in Acts (Acts 2:16–41, 42; 3:12–26; 4:2). The apostles did not expound Old Testament Scripture as their teaching. They declared the story and teaching of Jesus as the fulfillment of Scripture. Apostolic teaching mirrors Jesus' own teaching. Biblical quotations are frequently offered, of course, but only as evidence for the identity of the Messiah. As I have said, this is the sense in which "all Scripture . . . is *useful* for teaching" (2 Tim. 3:16).

## 3.2. "Teaching" in the Pastoral Epistles and Beyond

In Timothy's day, as we have noted, almost all of the apostolic traditions were oral—though, any apostolic writing that became available would be added to the tradition that Timothy was to lay down for others. There are good scriptural reasons (not just historical) for thinking of "teaching" in 1 Timothy 2:12 in this specific or technical sense. Once the history alerts us to the fact that there was no New Testament canon to expound in the mid-first century *and* that Paul was schooled in the oral traditions of the Pharisees, the numerous references to "teaching" in the Pastoral Epistles and elsewhere come into sharp focus. (This is the purpose of the historical study of the New Testament: not to reveal what isn't there in the text, but rather to focus our eyes properly to see what is there already.) I hope this becomes plain in what follows.

It could be argued that focusing on the Pastoral Epistles, rather than all of Paul's letters or, indeed, the whole New Testament, is a questionable strategy. Isn't that "stacking the deck" a little? Actually, it is common in New Testament studies to group letters 1 and 2 Timothy and Titus together. For some scholars, this grouping is partly because they argue that Paul did not write these letters. The language and theology in this literature are like each other but unlike the rest of Paul's letters. Other scholars, however, rightly reply that the differences, though real, should not be exaggerated and, in any case, all of them can be accounted for by the simple observation that these three epistles were written to authorized ministry colleagues (head pastors), not to churches. The letter I might write about church life to the Rev. Matthew Stedman, my friend and colleague at St Andrew's Roseville, would be quite different from the one I send to the wider congregation. I could assume a high level of theological education and use multiple technical terms. I would probably focus on church structures and staff issues and I would no doubt say a lot about the content and process of preaching.

This is exactly what we find in the Pastoral Epistles, and the language of "teaching" provides a clear example. The verb "to teach" (*didaskō*) occurs *slightly* more often in the three Pastoral Epistles than in the remaining ten epistles. The *nouns* for "teaching" (*didachē* and *didaskalia*), however, are strikingly prominent: 17 of Paul's 25 uses of "teaching" appear in just these three Pastoral Epistles. It is clearly a collection of literature with a special concern for teaching. It ought to be our main target, especially since it is here (1 Tim. 2:12) that we find our ban on women teaching men. I will expand this discussion to include Paul's other letters, but we should focus on the Pastoral Epistles. My claim will not be that every instance of "teaching" in Paul's writings has the same reference. After all, not every instance of "evangelize" (*euangelizomai*)—an obvious technical term for Paul—means "to tell the gospel" of Christ (cf. 1 Thess. 3:6). It will be enough to show that this is clearly the dominant usage in Paul's letters, especially in the Pastoral Epistles, and that this usage should shape our thinking about the prohibition in 1 Timothy 2:12.

I begin with the most extended treatment of the process of "teaching" in Paul's letters: 2 Timothy 1:11–2:2. The passage commences with a clear statement of the connection between *teaching* and the *fixed (oral) apostolic traditions*:

[For this gospel] I was appointed a preacher and apostle and teacher [*didaskalos*], which is why I suffer as I do. But I am not ashamed, for I know whom I have believed, and I am convinced that he is able to guard until that Day what has been entrusted to me. Follow the pattern of the sound words that you have *heard* from me, in the faith and love that are in Christ Jesus. By the Holy Spirit who dwells within us, guard the good *deposit* entrusted to you. (2 Tim. 1:11–14, italics added)

Paul describes himself as a "teacher" (as well a "preacher" and "apostle"), and then he urges Timothy to be the custodian of the teacher's words. These words are a fixed set of apostolic rulings and remembrances, a "deposit" entrusted to Timothy by word of mouth. A few verses later, Paul will use the verb "to deposit" with reference to the ministry of teachers (2 Tim. 2:2).

In the following paragraph (2 Tim. 1:15–18) Paul explains how some have rejected him (Phygelus and Hermogenes) and others have continued to be faithful to him (Onesiphorus). This sets up the crucial call in chapter 2 for Timothy to be one of the faithful ones—to take up the mantle of "teacher" and to ensure that the apostolic words entrusted to him are now passed onto other teachers. The meaning of "teaching" could hardly be clearer:

You then, my child, be strengthened by the grace that is in Christ Jesus, and what you have heard from me in the presence of many witnesses entrust to faithful men who will be able to *teach* [*didaskō*] others also. (2 Tim. 2:1–2, italics added)

"Teaching" here—surely the same as "teaching" in 1 Timothy 2:12—does not mean an *exposition* of a Bible passage. It means the careful process of laying down the fixed traditions first delivered by the apostle(s), the original teacher(s). Just as Paul was the great teacher (and Jesus before him), so Timothy is now to teach others who can teach. The "also" in "teach others also" makes clear that what Timothy was to do for these trainee teachers—lay down the entrusted words of the apostle—is the same as these new teachers were to do for others. Put another way, Paul had a "deposit" that he gave to Timothy (2 Tim. 1:14). Now Timothy is "to deposit" this material with other teachers: the word translated above "entrust" (*paratithēmi*) is the verb form related to the noun "deposit" (*parathēkē*) used a few verses earlier. It underlines the careful nature of oral transmission in the churches of Paul. After all, without a New Testament to read out, this depositing or teaching process was the central means of hearing what the apostles had said about the life and teaching of Jesus and about living in the new covenant.

In Titus 1:9 Paul speaks of the qualifications of an overseer, "He must hold firm to the trustworthy word as taught [*kata tēn didachēn*], so that he may be able to give instruction in sound doctrine [*didaskalia*] and also to rebuke those who contradict it." It would be difficult to read this passage as anything other than a description of the overseer's task to preserve the apostolic tradition and lay it down for others. The "trustworthy word" (*pistos logos*, 1:9) is not a collection of biblical expositions that elders are to remember. This is a recurring expression in the Pastoral Epistles (1 Tim. 1:15; 3:1; 4:9; 2 Tim. 2:11; Titus 3:8) that refers to a fixed set of new covenant messages that Paul had passed on to his apprentices and that they, in turn, are to lay down for the church.

The other key term Paul uses in Titus 1:9 is *didaskalia* ("teaching" or "doctrine"), which is clearly synonymous with the "trustworthy word." It usually means the *content* of what is taught. As Paul says in Romans 12:6–7: "Having gifts that *differ* according to the grace given to us, let us use them . . . the one who teaches [*didaskō*], in his teaching [*didaskalia*] (italics added.)" The term appears fifteen times in the Pastoral Epistles. One instance refers to "teachings" of demons (1 Tim. 4:1), but the rest refer to the content of the apostolic deposit. Like the verb "to teach," the noun "teaching" is clearly a technical term and is widely acknowledged. As I.

Howard Marshall puts it, *didaskalia* refers to "the approved, apostolic doctrine," and it underlines Paul's "emphasis on the concept of a fixed body of Christian doctrine."[35] In other words, all fourteen examples of this usage in the Pastoral Epistles (1 Tim. 1:10; 4:6, 13, 16; 5:17; 6:1, 3; 2 Tim. 3:10, 16; 4:3; Titus 1:9; 2:1, 7, 10) underline the central point of this chapter: "teaching," as a verb and a noun, refers not to Bible exposition but to the body of apostolic words that was to be repeatedly laid down for churches.

Reflection on such evidence led Klaus Wegenast in his study of teaching terminology in Paul to conclude that in the Pastoral Epistles, especially, *didaskō* means "to teach in the sense of handing down a fixed body of doctrine which must be mastered and then preserved intact."[36] The underlying account of teaching offered by Wegenast is widely assumed in New Testament scholarship, even if this hasn't had much influence on the way we talk about the connection between Paul's "teaching" and the contemporary "sermon."

With all of the above in mind, the crucial occurrence of the verb "to teach" in 1 Timothy 2:12 ("I do not permit a woman to teach") is most naturally read in the same way. Nothing in the verse itself tells us what "teach" means; it is the usage of this terminology in the Pastoral Epistles that gives us its likely sense. If these letters used the word "teach" to mean expounding Scripture or explaining and applying the message of Paul, we would have an alternative route. But "teaching" never has this sense. Rather, it means *to lay down the fixed body of apostolic words*.

There are four instances of "teaching" words in the build-up to 1 Timothy 2:12, and they provide a helpful backdrop for understanding the words in this crucial passage. The first two refer to sub-Christian or counterfeit-Christian "teaching." In 1:3 Paul says he wants Timothy to command certain men not "to teach any different doctrine" (a single word: *heterodidaskalō*), an odd prohibition that suggests there is a *correct* body of material to be taught and an *incorrect* body of material. This "teaching different doctrines" has to do with "myths" and "endless genealogies" (1:4) not bad expositions of Scripture.

Second, a few verses later (1:7), the apostle remarks that these heretics style themselves as "law-teachers" (*nomodidaskaloi*), a term that suggests they were part of a Jewish movement. Elsewhere in the New Testament, this term is only used of "the Pharisees and teachers of the law" who opposed Jesus (Luke 5:17) and of Gamaliel, Paul's own former teacher, who is described as "a Pharisee and teacher of the law" (Acts 5:34). These first two instances of "teaching"-vocabulary are *sub*-Christian. They nevertheless remind us of the Jewish context of "teaching" for Paul and stand in contrast to the teaching that Paul urges Timothy to promote. Again, this has little to do with expositions of Scripture and everything to do with the correct body of apostolic traditions.

In 1 Timothy 1:10–11 we find the third example of "teaching" terminology in the lead-up to 2:12. It is the first Christian use of the term—set over and against the parody of "teaching" found among the heretics. He speaks of "whatever else is contrary to sound doctrine [*didaskalia*, "teaching"], in accordance with the gospel of the glory of the blessed God with which I have been entrusted." Here it is clear not only that "teaching" concerns a fixed body of material but also that its content is defined by the *new covenant* gospel rather than Old Testament Scripture.

The same point is clear in the final use of "teaching" vocabulary in 1 Timothy, which appears just a few verses before Paul says that women may not teach men. In 2:5–7 he writes:

> For there is one God, and there is one mediator between God and men, the man Christ Jesus, who gave himself as a ransom for all, which is the testimony given at the proper time. For this I was appointed a preacher

and an apostle (I am telling the truth, I am not lying), a *teacher* [*didas-kalos*] of the Gentiles in faith and truth. (italics added)

Paul's description of himself as a new covenant preacher, apostle, and "teacher" has a close (and no doubt conscious) parallel in 2 Timothy 1:11–13, discussed above. There Paul writes, "for which [gospel] I was appointed a preacher and apostle and teacher. . . . Follow the pattern of the sound words that you have heard from me." Clearly, Paul's own ministry as "teacher" was defined by laying down the new covenant material entrusted to him, which was in turn entrusted to other teachers. This is the activity and authority that Paul restricts to certain men: "I do not permit a woman to teach or to exercise authority over a man" (2:12).

I am contending that nothing in Paul's usage of "teaching" in the Pastoral Epistles suggests this word means explaining or applying the text of Scripture. All of the evidence leads to the conclusion that he is referring to the high and holy task of preserving and passing on the apostolic traditions about Jesus. To recall my earlier analogy, the word "football" may have a broad meaning in Australia—including at least four sports—but it has only one meaning in the UK. Evangelicals have read into the word "teaching" a broad and multifaceted definition that does not sit well with Paul's specific usage in the Pastoral Epistles.

A similar sense of "teaching" is found elsewhere in Paul's letters. In Romans 6:17 he declares: "But thanks be to God, that you who were once slaves of sin have become obedient from the heart to the standard of teaching [*didachē*] to which you were committed." This cannot refer to a particular kind of exposition of a biblical text. It must mean that the Romans had received the apostolic traditions about Jesus some time before Paul wrote to them (in the late 50s). The same thought appears at the end of Romans: "Watch out for those who cause divisions and create obstacles contrary to the doctrine that you have been taught [*didachē*]" (Rom. 16:17); and again in Colossians 2:7: "rooted and built up in him [Jesus], just as you were taught [*didaskō*]."

Another interesting example appears in 1 Corinthians 4:17. Here, Paul speaks of what he "teaches" in all the churches, suggesting there is a defined and repeatable body of information he lays down everywhere:

> For though you have countless guides in Christ, you do not have many fathers. For I became your father in Christ Jesus through the gospel. I urge you, then, be imitators of me. That is why I sent you Timothy, my beloved and faithful child in the Lord, to remind you of my ways in Christ, as I teach [*didaskō*] them everywhere in every church. (1 Cor. 4:15–17)

In her published doctoral thesis on early Christian education, Claire Smith rightly says this passage "suggests there was a recognisable and distinct body of teaching that could be described as Paul's 'ways in Christ Jesus,' and his action of sending Timothy indicates a concern for ensuring this content was learned and observed."[37] She chides other specialists for suggesting that this idea of a fixed "teaching" only appears in Paul's *later* letters, such as the Pastoral Epistles. It is true this usage is especially apparent there—partly because "teaching" words are more frequent—but Smith is right to draw our attention to its clear presence in the earlier letter of 1 Corinthians.[38] Paul was a "traditionalist" with a fixed body of teaching from the beginning of his ministry (something his training as a Pharisee made easy).

Given that "teaching" for Paul consistently involves transmitting new covenant content (not Old Testament Scripture) *and* that there was no New Testament to expound when 1 Corinthians, Romans, and Colossians were penned, there is no avoiding the conclusion that "teaching" throughout these passages refers, as it does in the Pastoral Epistles, to laying down for congregations the material the apostles had passed on (mostly by word of mouth). In all of this, Paul's background as a Pharisee devoted to the "traditions of the fathers" is clear.

## 3.3. Teaching That Was Written Down

Fixed apostolic "teaching" was not only passed on in *oral* form. As I have already said, Paul's letters themselves also functioned as a form of delivering apostolic tradition. It is true that the vast majority of what a first-century Christian knew about Christ was received prior to reading any apostolic letters, but when those letters arrived, they supplemented that fixed body of knowledge.

The most obvious example is the apostolic letter sent to Gentile churches advising that they do not need to submit to circumcision (Acts 15:22–32). These believers already knew about Jesus' teaching, miracles, death and resurrection, and the importance of baptism and forming themselves into communities of faith. All of that came to them by oral tradition. The letter *added* to that tradition. Judas and Silas, who hand-delivered a copy of the apostolic letter, "encouraged [exhorted] and strengthened" the churches. Similarly, in 2 Thessalonians 2:15 Paul remarks, "So then, brothers, stand firm and hold to the traditions [*paradoseis*] that you were taught [*didaskō*] by us, either by our spoken word *or by our letter*" (italics added). Here Paul makes clear that his letter performs the function of *teaching* or *handing on the apostolic traditions*.

Some might say this means that an exposition of 2 Thessalonians must also be "teaching"; therefore, teaching and exposition are one. It would be more accurate, however, to describe an exposition of 2 Thessalonians as a *commentary on* the teaching or an *exhortation based on* the teaching—similar to Judas's and Silas's "exhortation" on the basis of the apostolic letter of Acts. It is not itself teaching in the sense Paul means here. In the apostle's usage "teaching," unlike explanation, encouragement, or exhortation, is fundamentally about the authoritative preservation and transmission of the fixed traditions of the apostles. A contemporary sermon contains far more (and, in a sense, far less) than that. *Some* contemporary sermons involve something close to authoritatively preserving and laying down the apostolic deposit, but I do not believe this is the typical function of the weekly exposition.

Numerous other references to "teaching" in Paul's letters fit the same general pattern, though less explicitly. For example, when Paul charges Timothy to "command and teach [*didaskō*] these things" in 1 Timothy 4:11, he is not asking him to expound passages of Scripture. He is asking him to preserve and repeat the things just mandated in Paul's letter to him. It is a command to add to the "apostolic deposit" the content of this part of the letter. It could be extrapolated from this that Timothy now has a responsibility to expound the letter itself to the churches in his care. In other words, "teach these things" would mean that Timothy should give expository sermons on this new apostolic letter. That is one possible extension of what Paul says.

A simpler reading takes Paul to mean that Timothy should communicate to the churches verbally the traditions laid down by Paul in this letter. There is no hint that Paul expected this piece of personal correspondence between master and apprentice to be read out loud, let alone expounded, to the Christians of Ephesus, where Timothy was serving, especially when so many of the encouragements, logistical instructions, and warnings in this letter are aimed directly at Timothy as the man in charge of the churches of Ephesus. When Paul says "teach these things," he means the things just mentioned, not the total content of the letter. Nothing here suggests that "teach" means *exegete and apply*; it means *repeat and lay down*.

Paul also instructs his protégé to "teach [*didaskō*] and urge these things" (1 Timothy 6:2b). Again, there is no indication this means that a sermon should be given on the letter. It just means that Timothy is to relay to the churches in his care the instructions Paul has just given concerning the behaviour of slaves and masters (6:1). Timothy literally had the authority, which only the teacher had, to *lay down for others* the apostolic information and commands that had been entrusted to him. That's what teaching was. Without it no one had access to the apostolic deposit.

I have no doubt that Timothy added to these apostolic teachings his own appeals, explanations, and applications, but these are not the constitutive or defining element of teaching. At that point, Timothy would be moving into what is more appropriately called "exhortation," similar to the exhortation that seems to have accompanied a reading of Old Testament Scripture. I am not creating a hard distinction between teaching and exhorting, but I am observing that, whereas teaching is principally about laying something down in fixed form, exhorting is principally about urging people to obey and apply God's truth. Remember, it is Paul who insists that teaching and exhorting (and prophesying) are "different functions" (Rom. 12:4–8). I am to highlight the difference by reflecting on how the New Testament, and especially Paul himself, uses these words.

"To teach" throughout the Pastoral Epistles (and elsewhere) means to preserve and lay down the apostolic traditions, either for the first time or the hundredth time. Usually, this refers to traditions laid down in oral form, but even when it refers to traditions laid down in a letter (2 Thess. 2:15; 1 Tim. 4:11), the idea is the same: authoritative teaching refers not to an exposition or application of the truth, whether in the Old Testament or an apostolic letter, but to the faithful transmission to others of the things declared by the apostles. Almost every instance of "teaching" in Paul has this in mind.[39]

Some may respond that *transmitting the traditions of the apostles* is precisely what a contemporary Bible exposition does. That may be true in a secondary sense, since whenever the New Testament is read and quoted (as in a sermon) an act of formal transmission is taking place. But the fact that a 300-word Bible passage usually inspires a 3,000-word sermon is proof enough that far more is going on in an exposition (and far *less*) than preserving and laying down the apostolic deposit. As I will explain in the final chapter, contemporary Bible exposition is certainly *connected* to what Paul meant by "teaching"—just as exhorting and prophesying are connected to "teaching"—but the two are not identical.

In his article arguing against women giving sermons, highly respected evangelical commentator Douglas J. Moo agrees that "teaching" refers to "the careful transmission of the (apostolic) tradition concerning Jesus Christ." He then adds that it *also* involves "the authoritative proclamation of God's will to believers in light of that tradition."[40] I accept the first and foundational part of the definition (most do), but the second part seems to be added without biblical warrant. It appears to be an attempt to secure the status of a modern sermon as "teaching." Moo is refuting the suggestion that exhortation *based on the teaching*—which is what sermons usually are—is less than teaching in the technical sense.

Rather, I am suggesting that a modern sermon is less a "careful transmission of the tradition concerning Jesus Christ" than it is an "authoritative proclamation of God's will to believers in light of that tradition." The former Paul labeled "teaching"; the latter he probably would have called "exhorting," maybe even "prophesying." No doubt there was a degree of teaching going on in exhorting and prophesying, just as there was some exhorting (and maybe prophesying) going on in teaching, but these activities were different enough in their constitutive elements, and levels of authority, for Paul to say they were different and to restrict the teaching ministry to certain trusted men.

When Paul refers to teaching in the technical and authoritative sense, he does not mean Bible exposition but preserving and repeating the apostolic deposit. While Paul was happy for women to engage in a range of public speaking activities, in 1 Timothy 2:12 he makes clear that "teaching" is a ministry only for certain handpicked men.[41] Paul's ruling is clear and binding, but it does not apply directly to what we call "sermons." Others have made similar arguments, including the stalwart Reformed evangelical theologian J. I. Packer:

> Teaching, in other words, is a different exercise today from what it was in Paul's day. I think it is an open question whether in our day Paul would have forbidden a woman to teach from the Bible . . . When you teach from the Bible, in any situation at all, what you are saying to people is, "Look, I am trying to tell you what it says. I speak as to wise men and women. You have your Bibles. You follow along. You judge what I say." No claim to personal authority with regard to the substance of the message is being made at all. It seems to me that this significant difference between teaching then and teaching now does, in fact, mean that the prohibition on women preaching and teaching need not apply.[42]

Packer's openness to women preaching, here and elsewhere in his writings, is based on the historic shift in authority (from the *teacher* to the *Bible*) that occurred when the apostolic "teaching" was finally codified in the canon of Scripture; teaching is therefore "a different exercise today" from what it was in Paul's day. I wholeheartedly agree, but I am offering the additional suggestion that what goes on in a typical sermon today is closer to what Paul called "the exhortation" (and maybe also "prophesying"), an activity he never restricted to men. Thus, for me, it is not just that no one today has quite the same authority as the ancient teacher—the walking repository of apostolic truth; it is that "teaching" never referred to expounding a biblical text and urging people in the power of the Spirit to heed its message.

I want to conclude this chapter with something of a thought experiment, an imaginative portrait of a first-century church service. It is largely speculative, but I hope it illustrates something of both kinds of speaking one might have encountered in a Pauline church and the heavy reliance early believers had on the teacher.

## 3.4. A First-Century Church Service (A Thought Experiment)

As the hymn proposed by Phoebe reached its climax, the group of 50 or so in her home was struck once again by the final lines:

> . . . at the name of Jesus every knee should bow,
> in heaven and on earth and under the earth,
> and every tongue confess that Jesus Christ is Lord,
> to the glory of God the Father. (Phil 2:10–11)

The apostle himself had taught them these words five or so years earlier, along with its ancient tune, "Doe of the Morning," a favourite from his days in the synagogue when he was tutored by the great Gamaliel in Jerusalem. Paul had taught them many such hymns (and tunes) as he laid down the apostles' traditions concerning the Lord Jesus.

After a brief time of silence, Crispus, the president of the meeting and one-time ruler of Corinth's synagogue, invited a young Demetrius to read one of the scrolls kept safe in a clay jar in Phoebe's cupboard. It contained a portion of the prophet Isaiah written in Greek. It was a favourite of the community, as it had been of their apostle. With the utmost seriousness Demetrius began reading:

The Lord says: "These people come near to me with their mouth and honor me with their lips, but their hearts are far from me. Their worship of me is made up only of rules taught by men. Therefore once more I will astound these people with wonder upon wonder; the wisdom of the wise will perish, the intelligence of the intelligent will vanish."

The reading continued for at least ten minutes, before Crispus motioned with his hand to Miriam. "Dear sister, please bring us a word of exhortation, if you would," conscious of her long association with the Scriptures as the daughter of an eminent family of the synagogue. Miriam was a widow and a deacon of the church of Cenchrea, just like Pheobe. Her main ministry was ensuring that the other widows were cared for in the daily food roster. Frequently, however, she was called upon to offer insights into the Scriptures of Israel.

"Brothers and sisters," Miriam said with a mix of grace and confidence, "the prophet calls on us not to follow mere human rules but to listen only to the word of the Lord. Here alone is where true wisdom is found. Our city philosophers think that they are wise and we are the foolish. They mock us for following the crucified one. Of course, on their definitions that is right. We are fools. But God has spoken and acted in his world, disclosing what the rational mind could never have discerned on its own. In my own family there are Pharisees of note. They too claim to be wise. They build a fence around the Torah, establishing rule after rule passed down from the fathers. They bind my people in traditions they themselves are unable to keep."

Miriam continued on like this for ten minutes or more, quoting Scripture from memory and anecdotes from her strict Jewish upbringing. "If I am not mistaken," she said as she concluded, "our Lord Jesus himself once accused Jewish teachers of placing heavy loads on their disciples and being unwilling to lift a finger to help them." Speaking more hesitantly, she added, "Indeed, I seem to recall that this very passage from Isaiah was quoted by our Lord." She paused. "Is that correct, Tertius?" She singled out the freedman whom Paul himself had chosen to remember the ways and words of the Lord. He stood up.

Tertius was an elderly gentleman whose dignified demeanor hid the scars of his former life as the slave and scribe of Claudius Lysias, a local port official. Tertius always conveyed thoughtfulness and trustworthiness, qualities the apostle always looked for in his appointed teachers. "Yes, dear sister," he said with real appreciation for her exhortation. "What you have said is right. Indeed, as I have it from the apostle, the Lord Jesus was once in debate with the Pharisees and teachers of the law who traveled from Jerusalem to Galilee to confront the master. They accused him and his apostles of not eating with clean hands in accordance with the traditions of their elders. Imagine that, teachers of falsehood daring to confront the Lord of all truth!"

He paused. The church sat eager to hear once again the Lord's words. "Then the Master quoted this very passage from Isaiah, 'They worship me in vain; their teachings are but rules taught by men.' He drove the point home, insisting that they had let go of the commands of God and were holding on to the traditions of men. He rebuked them for breaking the law of Moses concerning honouring father and mother by decreeing their resources 'corban,' that is, devoted to God and so not available to their parents. If I remember correctly, the Master concluded with the words, 'Thus you nullify the word of God by your tradition that you have handed down. And you do many things like that.'"

The statement was powerful, and several people in the meeting could be heard repeating the words—as if to brand them into their own memories—"You nullify the word of God by your tradition."

Tertius sat down and Crispus asked Miriam if she wanted to add anything. She did not. But Drusilla the prophetess stood where she was and waited for Cripus's invitation. "Speak, daughter of Mnason," he said. "Bring us something for our edification." The congregation was used to Drusilla's voice. Like the famous daughters of Philip the evangelist at Caesarea, she was well known for prophesying. Her words were always weighed by the elders but rarely did anyone believe she had spoken out of step with the teaching. Her words were brief but powerful, focusing everyone's attention on the danger that awaits all who follow false wisdom, whether that of the synagogue or the marketplace. "The sacred writings and the teachings of the apostles," she said in closing, "only these can save us from the coming wrath."

And with that Crispus led the congregation in prayer. He pleaded the Lord to keep this small community in the truth and to save many throughout Achaia. And he praised God for the faith once delivered to the saints. After a final hymn, Phoebe invited everyone to move to the banquet hall, where they shared another meal to remember the Lord's death until he comes.

# Part 4
# Teaching No More? How Modern Sermons and Ancient Teaching Are Connected

> **In a nutshell:** Even though the "apostolic deposit" is found only in the pages of the New Testament and no individual is charged with preserving and transmitting that information, contemporary sermons still play the vital role of commenting on the apostolic teaching (and various other parts of Scripture) and urging believers to apply God's Word to modern life. Sermons are closer to what Paul called "exhortation" than they are to what he called "teaching."

If we wholly equate the modern sermon with ancient "teaching" (*didaskō*), it makes sense to believe that women should be excluded from the pulpit (though we would still have to ponder why so few mechanisms are in place in evangelical circles today to encourage women to exhort, prophesy, and explain God's truth in church). However, both history and Scripture rule out the absolute identification of "teaching" with expository sermons. So, what is the connection between the two? And to what degree does "teaching" still exist today?

## 4.1. The Teaching Role of the New Testament Canon

If "teaching" in 1 Timothy 2:12 refers to preserving and laying down the traditions of the apostles, the warrant for thinking of modern preaching as the same as "teaching" is not strong. Frankly, no preacher today is an authorised repository of the apostolic deposit in the way that Timothy, Titus, and those they appointed were. That deposit is now preserved in the New Testament writings, not in individuals. Modern preachers *expound* the teaching and *exhort* believers to live in accordance with the teaching, but they do not preserve and transmit it to the same degree, in the same manner, or with the same authority. That role is performed by the New Testament text itself. Some "transmission" takes place during the sermon, whenever the New Testament is quoted, but that is a secondary function of the sermon. Prophesying and exhorting may also cite the apostolic traditions (the teachings now in the New Testament), but that doesn't turn these activities into teaching in the New Testament sense of the term.

There is a close Jewish parallel to this, mentioned earlier, that provides a historical illustration (if not an argument). The oral traditions preserved and passed on by the Pharisees—the material Jesus rejected as mere "human teachings" (Mark 7:7–13)—eventually became fixed in a document known as the Mishnah (ca. AD 200). This book is a collection of the rulings of about 120 rabbis from the first and second centuries, and it is regarded as the "Second Torah" by Judaism to this day. For most it is Scripture, not a mere compendium of historical rulings.

In a similar way, the apostolic traditions once preserved and laid down by teachers have come to be codified in the unchangeable form of documents, some of which were written by apostles (e.g., John, Paul, and Peter) and some by second-generation teachers (e.g., Mark, Luke, and the author of Hebrews). That apostolic deposit has been incorporated entirely into the New Testament text. For us, the New Testament *is* the apostolic deposit and therefore binding as Scripture.

In Paul's day, if you wanted to find out what Jesus had said about divorce, for example, you had to ask a teacher, and he would rehearse for you the specific sayings he had committed to memory (just as the Pharisees could repeat what Rabbi Hillel had said about divorce laws). The teacher's role was not so much to expound, illustrate, and apply those remembered sayings of Jesus; it was to preserve them as a fixed deposit and to lay them down as the basis of all Christian reflection. No doubt plenty of exposition and application of this material also took place in the churches (through teachers, prophets, and exhorters), but those ancillary activities are more appropriately described as exhorting and prophesying, since their core purpose is more about edification than preservation. This is why I have been saying that teaching, in the Pauline sense, never was "exposition" in the contemporary sense. Teaching is about preserving and laying down.

Today, of course, believers can go straight to the Gospels and read Jesus' words about divorce for themselves. No human being preserves and lays down the teachings of Jesus and the apostles in exactly the same way anymore. Maximum authority resides in Scripture more than any preacher and in the public Bible readings more than the sermon.[43] This, of course, does not mean that Paul's ban in 1 Timothy 2:12 prevents women today from reading the Bible publicly since no such reader is claiming to be the repository of the information they're reading out. They are simply *performing* the text, not preserving or laying it down.

It could be argued that using the production of the New Testament canon as a reason not to obey the clear command of a New Testament text (1 Tim. 2:12) is inconsistent. But that would be to misunderstand my argument. The key point is not that we no longer need to prevent women from expounding God's truth now that we have it in a written form. What I am saying is that "teaching" in 1 Timothy 2:12 never referred to "expounding God's truth." It only meant preserving and laying down what the apostles had declared about the new covenant: "What you have heard from me in the presence of many witnesses entrust to faithful men who will be able to *teach* others also" (2 Tim. 2:2, italics added). First Timothy 2:12 never rightly stood in the way of women delivering Spirit-empowered speeches for the edification of the church. Nowhere in Scripture are they prevented from exhorting, prophesying, evangelizing, and so on. The point, therefore, is not that women can now "teach" because we have a fixed New Testament. Rather, it is that teaching never involved the many and varied things we do in a sermon.

In essence, I am questioning whether the typical sermon today performs a task equivalent to that of ancient teaching. Contemporary preachers perform a role *analogous* to that of the ancient teacher, but analogy is not equivalence. We have taken an instruction Paul gave concerning a specific speaking ministry and have *universalised* it to apply to all sustained, biblical public speaking in church. Paul did not do this. Authoritative "teaching" is the only speaking activity he restricted to (certain qualified) men.

## 4.2. What Is a Modern Exposition?

Modern expositors *comment on* the teaching, *exhort* us to heed the teaching, and *apply* the teaching to modern life—all in the power of the Spirit. To be clear, this is a comment about the *form* of the sermon. Much more can and should be said about the *theology* of sermons, but this is not the place for that. Contemporary sermons are certainly related to ancient teaching, but they are more related to what Paul called prophesying (*prophēteuō*), preaching (*kēryssō*), and, especially, exhorting (*parakaleō*). These activities are not restricted to men. No doubt these ministries carry *some* "authority" and should be performed by trustworthy people, but it is not the same authority that was invested in the first-century teacher, without whom there was no reliable access to the apostolic deposit.

The Spirit speaks to his people through prophesying, preaching, and exhortation. There is therefore a dimension of authority in all of these activities; it just isn't the authority Paul restricts to certain men in 1 Timothy 2:12. After all, "authority" is not binary, as if "'teaching" turns the switch ON and every other type of speaking turns it OFF. We must recognise that Paul saw authority on a spectrum. In connection with prophecy, Paul says we should "weigh what is said" (1 Cor. 14:29). This doesn't mean the woman who prophesied in Corinth had no authority at all. It means that her words, like those of any male prophet, had to be assessed against the *authoritative teaching*. If their words were judged to be in conformity with the apostolic deposit, the church was to receive them as a message from the Lord. They were authoritative in a derivative and secondary sense (just like a typical modern sermon).

In Paul's day, and for at least a generation after him, the last port of call in any such weighing process was the teachers. There was no New Testament text to consult. Teachers themselves were not subject to this "weighing" process. Their authority was maximal. Unless you could find an apostle or a direct apostolic representative like Timothy, there was no way to "weigh" the words of the teacher.[44] This may help explain why Paul, who believed in the equality and complementarity of the sexes but not their symmetry, would reserve this maximal authority to male teaching elders, while happily inviting women to participate in other valuable speaking ministries designed for the building up of the church.

How wonderfully different is the situation of churches today! The words of the modern preacher are more like a *commentary* on Scripture and an *application* of Scripture (again, I am only describing the *form* of the sermon, not its theological significance). Modern preachers' comments, unlike the teachings of ancient teachers, can and should be "weighed." After all, at least 90 percent of the words coming out of their mouths are *theirs*, not the apostles'. They are subject to the teaching found in Scripture itself.[45] Evangelicals rightly train their congregations to weigh what the preacher says, and in this there is an implicit admission of the difference the canonization process has made to church life. Sermons are, in this sense at least, similar to the "weighed prophecies" of 1 Corinthians 14.

## 4.3. Missing New Testament Roles?

When I first began to think through the difference between ancient teaching and modern sermons, it troubled me that a role Paul describes in Scripture ("teaching") may no longer have a *precise* equivalent. How significant is this? Let me offer a few reflections on this question before clarifying the degree to which I think "teaching" does continue today.

Most evangelicals are comfortable with the thought that "apostles," for instance, have little or no modern counterpart, even though the New Testament makes clear that more people than the "Twelve" were called apostles (Acts 14:14; Rom. 16:7; 1 Cor. 12:28). Apostles may have an analogy in modern missionaries, but few of us would consider the two roles identical. Similarly, many of my Reformed colleagues feel this way about "prophesying." It was a foundational gift, they argue, not an enduring feature of the church through history. They say this knowing full well that "prophesying" was the main form of public speaking in church that Paul encourages in 1 Corinthians 12–14.

"Evangelists," too, have often been thought to be engaged in a ministry that is no longer active in the church. The great church leader Eusebius,[46] for instance, and my theological hero John Calvin, both thought "evangelists" were a thing of the past. Calvin wrote that the role of evangelists was "not established in the church as permanent," but was rather "only for that time during which

churches were to be erected where none existed before."[47] I think
Calvin is mistaken. My point, though, is that in the history of the
church, many have happily concluded that not every New Testament function has a precise contemporary counterpart. The same
may be said about "teachers" (in the strict sense intended by Paul).
I call myself a "Bible teacher," but I do so with a clear sense of the
differences, as well as the similarities, between the teachers in Paul's
letters and myself.

There are other ministries authorised in the Pastoral Epistles that
have "morphed" in the modern church. Consider Paul's clear direc-
tives about the "widows roll/roster," a ministry of care for the elderly:

> Let a widow be enrolled if she is not less than sixty years of age, having
> been the wife of one husband, and having a reputation for good works: if
> she has brought up children, has shown hospitality, has washed the feet
> of the saints, has cared for the afflicted, and has devoted herself to every
> good work. But refuse to enroll younger widows, for when their passions
> draw them away from Christ, they desire to marry. (1 Tim. 5:9–11)

The "widows roll/roster" continued on as a ministry of the churches
for at least two centuries after Paul gave these instructions, and
then it dwindled.[48] But no one today frets about the absence of this
ministry in our church structures. We acknowledge that what Paul
is mandating here—care for the elderly and vulnerable—has been
absorbed into the various social services of the church.

In a similar way, what Paul was mandating in his injunctions
about "teaching" in the Pastoral Epistles was the careful transmission of the apostolic deposit itself. That does continue today, in a
greatly improved manner, whenever the New Testament is repro-
duced and read. It also has an important "echo" as preachers exhort
congregations to embrace and apply the teaching now found in
Scripture. The role of the ancient teacher has been transposed, not
abolished. It continues, but mostly in a different key.

The sermon certainly has a crucial place in the Christian gathering, especially when the method is exposition. I also think that *some* transmission of the apostolic deposit still goes on in every decent sermon, in some more than others. In this sense, sermons are connected to what Paul called teaching, just as they are connected with what he called exhorting and prophesying, activities that Paul does not restrict just to men. I therefore find no strong reason to exclude women from the pulpit.

# Conclusion: Three (or Four) Responses

Let me offer a brief seven-point summary of my argument and then offer some imagined responses.

1. Paul mentions many different types of public speaking: prophesying, teaching, admonishing, reading, exhorting, evangelising, and preaching. They are all different words, depicting different activities.

2. In Romans 12 and elsewhere Paul makes clear that, whatever similarities there may be between these activities, they are "different" forms/functions of speaking (at least teaching, prophesying, and exhorting are different).

3. In 1 Timothy 2:12 Paul clearly states that he does not permit women to "teach" men. No other speaking activity is mentioned here. And the "authority" mentioned here is teaching-authority or (less plausibly) a reference to the broader authority of being an elder.

4. Paul nowhere forbids women to engage in preaching, admonishing, exhorting, evangelising, reading, or prophesying. Indeed, in 1 Corinthians 11 it is clear he expects women to be prophesying in church. "Teaching" is the only restricted activity.

5. "Teaching" in Paul's usage, especially in the Pastoral Epistles, consistently refers to the task of passing on the "deposit" of apostolic words in a period when those words were mostly not written down. In all of this, Paul's Jewish background is clear, since Pharisees were well-known for preserving and passing on

a vast body of non-written material known as "the traditions of the fathers."

6. No text of the New Testament, including Paul's writings, says that "teaching" (*didaskō*, 1 Tim 2:12) is an exposition and application of a scriptural passage (i.e., what we call a sermon).

7. What we call "giving a sermon" has more in common with what Paul called "exhorting" and "prophesying'" than with what he labeled "teaching." The "word of exhortation" seems to have been a standard expression for a speech following an authoritative text.

Therefore, woman ought to be allowed to give sermons in our churches, without fearing that 1 Timothy 2:12 is being violated.

I have probably overlooked some evidence and counterarguments, and I hope I will receive corrections and criticisms cheerfully.[49] In order to invalidate the broader argument of this book, however, I feel two things need to be presented. First, critics will need to lay out an alternative understanding of *teaching authority* in 1 Timothy 2:12 that fits with the historical and biblical data. It cannot just be assumed. The "plain sense" reading fails as an argument if it cannot be shown that "teaching" in the New Testament refers to the things we normally do in a modern sermon.

Nor will it be enough to insist that we stick with the broad definition of teaching as *transmitting truth from one person to another*. Such a definition would only be useful if our goal were to add up all the occurrences of "teaching" in the Bible and come up with a definition broad enough to cover all of them at once. That might be how a dictionary entry begins, but it is not the way to discern the meaning of particular words in particular contexts. The broad definition of "teaching" is true; it just isn't accurate. It does not accurately describe Paul's usage, especially in the Pastoral Epistles.

I think it is indisputable that "teaching" does (consistently, if not exclusively) refer to the apostolic deposit authoritatively transmitted. To undermine the case I put forward, then, others would need to demonstrate examples of Christian "teaching" in the Pastoral Epistles—and there are many instances of the terminology—that *clearly do not* refer to the transmitted apostolic deposit, and then they would need to show why this usage fits 1 Timothy 2:12 better than the one I am proposing. It is true that there are examples of "otherwise teaching" or "teachings of demons," but these are only described as a type of "teaching" because they are parodies or perversions of Christian teaching. Thus, while Christian "teaching" in the Pastoral Epistles *clearly* does refer to passing on the apostolic deposit, I cannot find a single occurrence of the terminology where it clearly does not.

Second, a cogent argument will have to be made for equating modern sermons with *teaching* rather than with one of the other types of public speaking listed in the New Testament (such as exhortation) that are not restricted to men. This second challenge will prove especially difficult. Even if someone suggested that teaching in 1 Timothy 2:12 referred to something other than repeating and laying down the apostolic traditions, they would still have to explain why our church services rarely create opportunities for women to offer messages of exhortation, explanation, prophecy, or evangelism. The use of the word "teaching" in evangelical parlance to cover most types of sustained, biblical speech in church (and, for some, even the leading or emceeing of the service) is not justified.

I anticipate three broad responses to this short book (apart from outright rejection). Some may only accept the main point made in chapter 1, that there are numerous different speaking activities listed in the New Testament and only one of them is restricted to men. As a result, some may decide (afresh) to find ways to give women more of a voice in the church service, inviting them to give "talks," or whatever we call them, designed to strengthen the faith of those present. I would be delighted with such a response and am glad to report that, independent of this book, some churches in my own Sydney Anglican context are doing this.

Others may embrace my entire argument and conclude that no one "teaches" any more in the sense mentioned in 1 Timothy 2:12 and that explaining and applying a biblical text is never called "teaching" in the New Testament. Rather, that activity is closer to "exhorting" (or "prophesying"). As a result, *all* sermons are open to suitable men and women. I think this is a plausible application of the biblical data. The only awkwardness that would remain is the one confronting those who think "prophesying" no longer exists: What do we do with the passages that read as though "teaching" will be an ongoing ministry of the church? There are several ways to respond, but it is a question to be faced.

A third response (closer to my own current thinking) may conclude that, although the modern sermon cannot *always* be equated with what Paul calls "teaching" in 1 Timothy 2:12, *some* sermons today may be close analogies to the careful transmission of the apostolic deposit. On this view, sermons are seen on a spectrum: some are more like prophesying and exhorting and aim to urge obedience to Scripture or encourage confidence in God's truth; others function more as a focused mandating of apostolic doctrine.

According to this view "exhorting" sermons would be open to suitable men and women alike. But what about "teaching" sermons? This is an open question. It depends on the degree to which one sees teaching authority residing in the preacher today or in the text of the Bible. J. I. Packer, quoted above, holds that teaching authority has shifted from the teacher to the text. I assume this means that even sermons at the "mandating-of-apostolic-doctrine" end of the spectrum would be open to women, because although the activity itself broadly corresponds to ancient "teaching," the *authority* contained in the activity is not the same. As Packer remarks, "When you teach from the Bible, in any situation at all, what you are saying to people is, 'Look, I am trying to tell you what it says. I speak as to wise men and women. You have your Bibles. You follow along. You judge what I say.' No claim to personal authority with regard to the substance of the message is being made at all."[50] This is a reasonable line of argument.

With that said, I continue to think that Paul expected preaching itself to reflect the complementarity of the sexes. Adam was charged with being the protector of the first divine deposit; male elder-teachers are charged with preserving the last divine deposit. Packer preserves this complementarity by restricting the priesthood to men (in his Anglican context). However, Paul seemed to want congregational preaching, not just congregational structures, to embody God's complementary design for male-female relationships (otherwise, his simultaneous acceptance of women prophesying and restriction of their teaching makes little sense). Hence, it is my opinion that sermons at the "mandating-of-apostolic-doctrine" end of the spectrum—which I believe is *not* the typical Sunday sermon—ought to be preached by the male Senior Minister.

It will perhaps be frustrating to some that I don't intend to offer any examples of what such sermons involve. This is partly because my own thoughts are not fully formed and partly because I don't want to be overly prescriptive. I would prefer readers made up their own minds about how to apply the biblical data in our modern context. It is plain that the activity and authority Paul did not allow women in 1 Timothy 2:12 is not the same as exhorting and prophesying, activities he did not restrict to men. It is further clear that modern sermons are typically more like exhortation than laying down the apostolic deposit ("teaching"). Beyond this, we are in the realm of practical wisdom rather than theological obligation.

Those who share my conclusions will probably also find themselves wondering how the biblical principle of male responsibility might determine the relative frequency of men and women in the preaching roster. Again, I have no particular wisdom worth sharing. I raise it as a question I myself consider. I will say, however, that perhaps one close analogy to ancient teaching is the *design of the church's Bible teaching program itself.* How so? The person who shapes what the church hears as apostolic truth—the right balance of Old and New Testament material, the appropriate topical and evangelistic diet, the proper doctrinal emphases, and so on—is assuming the *maximum* teaching authority in the congregation. If anyone is preserving and laying down the apostolic deposit, it is such an individual. Happily, since the publication of the first edition of this book, the Rev Andrew Judd, grandson of Donald Robinson (who first alerted me to the connection between "teaching" and the apostolic deposit), reported to me that this former Anglican Archbishop of Sydney once speculated that the closest modern analogy to the ancient teacher *might* be the person responsible for preparing the sermon roster. Robinson was only musing, something for which he was well known, but I find the logic compelling.

I will leave it to readers to judge for themselves which of these three (or four) responses with their various permutations best reflects the teaching of God's Word. I myself have lingering questions about the ministry of women in the New Testament and today, and I continue to ponder them. What I no longer doubt, however, is that trained and godly women should be allowed to give sermons in our churches.

# Discussion Questions

## 1. Teaching Isn't Everything: What 1 Timothy 2:11–12 Cannot Mean

1. In your own words, summarise the author's argument so far. Is there anything you found confusing or that you disagreed with?

2. What would you say is the purpose of a "sermon"? How does it differ from the purpose of some of the other speaking activities listed in this chapter?

3. How could your church or small group enhance the opportunities for women to "prophesy" and "exhort"?

## 2. Laying It Down: What Teaching Really Is

1. In your own words, what is "teaching" (in the technical sense), according to the author? What are the historical arguments for this understanding?

2. Some may protest that the author relies too heavily on "historical background" inaccessible to the average reader? Do you agree? Why or why not?

3. Conduct a small "thought experiment": describe, if you can, what might have been different about Christian life and church gatherings in the period *before* there was a written New Testament (i.e., between AD 30 and 100).

## 3. Explain and Apply: How Exposition Differs from Teaching

1. The author says that "exposition of a Bible passage" is never referred to in the New Testament as "teaching," and yet he insists that this is still a God-honouring method of contemporary preaching. How do you react to these twin claims? Are they compatible with each other?

2. Please reread 2 Timothy 1:13–14 and 2:2. From these passages, how would you define what Paul means by teaching?

3. Why does the author believe "teaching" and "sermons" are not the same thing? What are some potential weaknesses in this argument?

## 4. Teaching No More? How Modern Sermons and Ancient Teaching Are Connected

1. Does the thought that a New Testament ministry (teaching) has no *precise* counterpart today trouble you? Why or why not? How does the author come to terms with this?

2. Thinking of your own church, does the Sunday service invite women's voices to be heard to the degree reflected in Scripture? What could be done to enhance or correct your church's regular practice?

3. Has this book changed your opinion on anything the Bible says about the different types of public speaking in church? If so, how?

## Conclusion: Three (or Four) Responses

1. In the concluding paragraphs the author describes three (or four) possible responses to the argument of the book. Discuss the merits and/or limits of each.

2. Whatever your view on women giving sermons, what can be done to create more open and generous discussion of the issue with those who see things differently?

# Endnotes

1. If pushed, I would admit to being a broad complementarian. I believe Scripture endorses a range of public speaking ministries for women, while maintaining the principle of male responsibility in church and the home.

2. Given that prayer and prophecy *in the church service* are topics of extended discussion in 1 Corinthians 12–14, it is unlikely that Paul is referring to something different in chapter 11. So also D. A. Carson, "Silent in the Churches: The Role of Women in 1 Corinthians 14:33b–36," in *Recovering Biblical Manhood and Womanhood* (ed. John Piper and Wayne Grudem; Wheaton, IL: Crossway, 2006), 133–47.

3. Numerous commentators rightly take "in the gospel" in Phil. 4:3 as a reference to gospel proclamation. So G. F. Hawthorne, *Philippians* (WBC 43; Dallas, 1983), 180; and P. T. O'Brien, *The Epistle to the Philippians* (NIGTC; Grand Rapids: Eerdmans, 1991), 481. On the women as evangelists in Philippi, see also Nils A. Dahl, "Euodia and Syntyche and Paul's Letter to the Philippians," in *The Social World of the First Christians: Essays in Honor of Wayne A. Meeks* (ed. L. Michael White and O. Larry Yarborough; Minneapolis: Fortress, 1995), 3–15. The comment of John Chrysostom (ad 347–407) that "these women seem to me to be the chief of the Church which was there" (*Homilies on Philippians no. 13*) goes further than the evidence allows but picks up the same hints.

4. Claudia V. Camp, "Huldah," in *Women in Scripture* (ed. Carol Meyers; Grand Rapids: Eerdmans, 2000), 96.

5. See, for example, Richard Kroeger and Catherine Kroeger, *I Suffer Not a Woman: Rethinking 1 Timothy 2:11–15 in Light of Ancient Evidence* (Grand Rapids: Baker, 1992). I am not persuaded by the kind of evidence and methodology offered in a book like this. A more measured and mainstream argument that verse 12 applies only to the problems of first-century Ephesus and "lacks any sense of universal imperative for all situations" (77) is offered by the great evangelical commentator Gordon Fee, *1 and 2 Timothy, Titus* (NIBC; Peabody, MA: Hendrickson 1988), 72–77. Fee's exegetical arguments are substantial, but I remain unpersuaded by them.

6. Anthony Thiselton, *The First Epistle to the Corinthians* (NIGTC; Grand Rapids: Eerdmans, 2000), 826.

7. See the detailed and measured discussion in David Peterson, "Prophetic Preaching in the Book of Acts," in *Serving God's Words: Windows on Preaching and Ministry* (ed. Paul A. Barker et al.; Nottingham, UK: Intervarsity Press, 2011), 53–74. Also see the paper by Mark Burkill, David Peterson, and Simon Vibert, "Ministry Work Group Statement concerning the Ministry of Women in the Church Today" (London: Latimer Trust, 2001).

8. The Greek is *proseche tē anagnōsei, tē paraklēsei, tē didaskalia.* "The use of the article with each of the three following nouns," writes I. Howard Marshall, a leading evangelical New Testament scholar, "indicates that these are familiar, recognised activities in the congregational meeting" (*The Pastoral Epistles* [ICC; London: T&T Clark, 2004], 562).

9. Ibid., 563.

10. Claire Smith, *Pauline Communities as Scholastic Communities: A Study of the Vocabulary of 'Teaching' in 1 Corinthians, 1 and 2 Timothy and Titus* (WUNT 335; Tübingen: Mohr Siebeck, 2012), 61.

11. See, for example, the excellent discussions of the technical quality of "teaching" vocabulary in Philip H. Towner, *The Letters to Timothy and Titus* (Grand Rapids: Eerdmans, 2006), 129–31, and in the same author's *The Goal of Our Instruction: The Structure of Theology and Ethics in the Pastoral Epistles* (JSNTSup 34; Sheffield Academic, 1989), 215. See also Robert Saucy, "Paul's Teaching on the Ministry of Women," in *Women and Men in Ministry: A Complementary Perspective* (ed. Robert Saucy and Judith K. Tenelshof; Chicago: Moody Press, 2001), 291–310. Saucy, a systematic theology professor from Talbot Seminary, comes to a different modern application of the material from my own, but his detailed account of the meaning of *didaskein* in the Pastoral Epistles is the same.

12. What is the connection here between teaching and authority? Some think Paul is making two separate rulings in 1 Timothy 2:11–12: (1) women are not allowed to teach; (2) women are not allowed to have any kind of authority over a man (e.g., William D. Mounce, *Pastoral Epistles* [WBC 46; Nashville: Nelson, 2000], 310–11). I think that is possible, and it doesn't really affect my argument either way, but the structure of the verses strongly suggests that the apostle is talking about one thing from two angles: *teaching authority* or the *authority that goes with teaching.* (Note: this is different from the argument of some that Paul is only referring to *really authoritative teaching* rather than *normal teaching.*) The logical progression of thought seems clear:

(Introduction): Let a woman learn quietly with all submissiveness.

(Instruction): I do not permit a woman to teach or to exercise authority over a man.

(Conclusion): Rather, she is to remain quiet.

Notice that "learning" and "submissiveness" in the introductory line are not two separate items but one: *submissive learning*. This sets up the explicit instruction that follows: "I do not permit a woman to teach or to exercise authority over a man." Given that the introductory statement refers to one thing from two angles, it seems natural to read the instruction that follows as again referring to one thing from two angles. He is contrasting *submissive learning* with the *authority of teaching* or *teaching-authority*. There is no doubt that Greek constructions using "and/or/nor" frequently have this sense. Grammatically, this is known as a *hendiadys*, as in the English expression "nice *and* warm," which describes a comfortable state from two perspectives. Many interpret "teach or exercise authority" in this way (see, e.g., Marshall, *The Pastoral Epistles*, 460).

The reading is confirmed by the conclusion to the command: "Rather, she is to remain quiet." Notice how the doublet "to teach or to exercise authority" is negated by just one idea, "to remain quiet," rather than two ideas, "to remain quiet *and* be submissive." Paul is not saying that women must not teach *and* that they must not have any other kind of authority. He is saying that women are not to have *teaching authority*, i.e., the authority to teach. I am not saying Paul is distinguishing between authoritative teaching and regular teaching. All "teaching," in the technical sense used throughout the Pastoral Epistles, is authoritative because with no New Testament yet in existence when Paul wrote to Timothy, the teacher was the last port of call for apostolic doctrine. With respect to this particular role, women are to practice "quietness" or "submissiveness." I should point out that "quietness" and "submissiveness" are not derogatory or patriarchal terms. Elsewhere, they are applied to Christians generally, men and women alike (Eph. 5:21; 1 Tim. 2:2).

13. The Westminster Confession of Faith 1.7. "All things in Scripture are not alike plain in themselves, nor alike clear unto all; yet those things which are necessary to be known, believed, and observed for salvation, are so clearly propounded, and opened in some place of Scripture or other, that not only the learned, but the unlearned, in a due use of the ordinary means, may attain unto a sufficient understanding of them."

14. Some might offer 1 Tim. 5:18 as evidence that the gospel of Luke was available by the time 1 Timothy was written: "For the Scripture says, 'You shall not muzzle an ox when it treads out the grain,' and, 'The laborer deserves his wages.'" The saying about the "laborer" also appears in Luke 10:7 on the lips of Jesus. Most scholars think that this is a citation either of oral tradition (which no doubt had the authority of Scripture) or of a document that predates Luke's gospel, usually designated Q. It is certain that Paul knew sayings of Jesus and passed them on to his churches (see, e.g., his reminder of the words of the Last Supper in 1 Cor. 11:23–25, which closely resembles Luke 22:19–22). Either way, the quotation in 1 Tim. 5:18 does not provide a good reason to think that the gospel of Luke was written before the 60s. See further: Mounce, *Pastoral Epistles*, 310–11; Marshall, *Pastoral Epistles*, 616–17. In all of this, I am not denying the suggestion of some scholars that parts of Jesus' teaching were written down in "notes" from an earlier period, perhaps even during his lifetime. See Rainer Riesner, "Jesus as Preacher and Teacher," in *Jesus and the Oral Gospel Tradition* (Sheffield: Sheffield Academic, 1991), 195–96.

15. D. A. Carson and Douglas J. Moo, *An Introduction to the New Testament* (2nd ed.; Grand Rapids: Zondervan; Leicester, UK: Inter-Varsity Press, 2005).

16. Important books on oral tradition in Judaism and early Christianity include Henry Wansbrough, ed., *Jesus and the Oral Gospel Tradition* (Sheffield: Sheffield Academic, 1991); Birger Gerhardsson, *The Reliability of the Gospel Tradition* (Peabody, MA: Hendrickson, 2001); James D. G. Dunn, *Jesus Remembered* (Grand Rapids: Eerdmans, 2003), esp. 173–254. For the fundamental importance of oral tradition in ancient Judaism, see the massive study by Catherine Hezser, *Jewish Literacy in Roman Palestine* (TSAJ; Tübingen: Mohr Siebeck, 2001). She is far more skeptical than I am about the accuracy of Jewish oral culture, but she lays out the compelling evidence that ancient Jews, despite having a book at the centre of their worship (the Torah or Old Testament), were profoundly oral, not literary, in their approach to culture and religion.

17. Mishnah *Berakot* 5:5. The *Mishnah*, as I will discuss, is a compilation of Jewish tradition written about AD 200.

18. Josephus, *Antiquities of the Jews* 13.297. Note what Josephus says about himself in his autobiography: "In my nineteenth year I began to govern my life by the rules of the Pharisees, a sect having points of resemblance to that which the Greeks call the Stoic school" (*Life*, 12).

19. Joachim Schaper, "The Pharisees," in *The Cambridge History of Judaism (vol.3): The Early Roman Period* (ed. William Horbury et al.; Cambridge: Cambridge University Press, 1999), 409.
20. Ibid., 421.
21. Mishnah *Abot* 1:1–16. The translation is that of Herbert Danby, *The Mishnah* (Oxford: Oxford University Press, 1933), 446–47.
22. Schaper, "The Pharisees," 421. A good illustration of the written and oral parts of Pharisaic tradition is found in a Greek inscription dedicating one of the synagogues of Jerusalem: "Theodotos son of Vettenos, priest and synagogue-ruler . . . built the synagogue for the reading of the Law and the teaching of the commandments [*eis didachēn entolōn*]." The inscription is dated to the late first century BC or early first century AD, i.e., to precisely the New Testament period (see Hannah M. Cotton, Werner Eck, et al., eds, *Corpus Inscriptionum: Iudaeae/Palestinae. Vol.1: Jerusalem, Part 1:1-704*, no.9 [Berlin: De Gruyter, 2010], 53). It is possible that "teaching of the commandments" refers to *exposition* of the written law (Old Testament) *following* the reading, even if "commandments" is not an apt description of the bulk of the Old Testament. Jewish specialists Martin Hengel, Roland Deines, and Joachim Schaper offer another interpretation. Theodotus built the synagogue for the "reading" of the written Torah and the "teaching" of the oral commandments—the bulk of the Pharisaic oral tradition was indeed made up of regulations. Given the presence of Pharisees in Jerusalem and their dominance generally in the synagogues, this is a compelling explanation of the Theodotus inscription. See Martin Hengel and Roland Deines, "E. P. Sanders' 'Common Judaism,'" *JTS* 46 (1995): 1–70, esp. pages 33–34; Schaper, "The Pharisees," 421–22. The arguments of these scholars are set against the views of E. P. Sanders ("Did the Pharisees Have Oral Law?" in *Jewish Law from Jesus to the Mishnah: Five Studies* (Phillipsburg, NJ: Trinity Press International, 1990), 97–130) that Pharisees did not dominate the synagogue and did not ascribe Torah-status to their oral tradition. Apart from the various historical arguments that can be mounted, the evidence of the Gospels (which Sanders tends to dismiss as secondary) clarifies both points (Mark 7:1–13; 12:38–39; Matt. 23:2; Luke 11:43; John 12:42). In any case, it is worth noting that the same two activities mentioned in the Theodotus synagogue inscription, "reading" and "teaching," feature also in Paul's instruction to Timothy, "Until I come, devote yourself to the public *reading*, to [the] exhortation, [and] to [the] *teaching*" (1 Tim. 4:13, italics added). As I will explain later,

this refers to the reading of the Old Testament, an exhortation based on the reading (which also took place in the synagogues) and the teaching, or laying down, of the apostolic oral tradition.

23. In decreasing order of strictness Mishnah *Gittin* 9:10 lists the ancient rabbis' rulings on divorce: "The House of Shammai say, 'A man should divorce his wife only because he has found grounds for it in unchastity, since it is said, *Because he has found in her indecency in anything (Deuteronomy 24:1).*' And the House of Hillel say, 'Even if she spoiled his dish, since it is said, *Because he has found in her indecency in anything.*' Rabbi Aqiba says 'Even if he found someone else prettier than she, since it is said, *And it shall be if she find no favor in his eyes* (Deuteronomy 24:1)." Against such a background, Jesus declared: "But I tell you that anyone who divorces his wife, except for sexual immorality, causes her to become an adulteress, and anyone who marries the divorced woman commits adultery" (Matt. 5:32; Mark 10:11; Luke 16:18). The disciples remembered Jesus' rulings, just as the Pharisees remembered Hillel's.

24. For an up-to-date discussion of the importance of authority figures within the oral traditioning process, see Richard Bauckham, *Jesus and the Eyewitnesses* (Grand Rapids: Eerdmans, 2006), 240–318.

25. Dunn, *Jesus Remembered*, 176–77. Similarly, Walter Liefeld remarks: "Christian teachers were involved in a most significant and sensitive task, that of transmitting the traditions of Jesus and of the early apostles" (Walter Liefeld, "Response to David M. Scholer's 1 Timothy 2:9–15 and the Place of Women in the Church's Ministry," in *Women, Authority and the Bible* [ed. Alvera Mickelsen; Downers Grove, IL: InterVarsity Press, 1986], 223). See also Joseph Fitzmyer, "The Office of Teaching in the Christian Church according to the New Testament," in Paul C. Empie et al., eds., *Teaching Authority and Infallibility in the Church* (Minneapolis: Augsburg, 1980), 186–212; Robert Saucy, "Paul's Teaching on the Ministry of Women," 291–310.

26. In a similar way, in Hebrews 5:12–6:2 the writer makes clear that the "teacher" (*didaskalos*) was the one who had "taught" (*didaskō*) the recipients "the basic principles of the oracles of God," or what he then calls "the elementary doctrine of Christ." With admonishing irony, he says that the recipients ought to be teachers themselves by now, but instead they seem to require re-teaching. He describes the process and content of this teaching in the next lines: "laying again a foundation of repentance from dead works and of faith toward God, and of instruction about washings, the

laying on of hands, the resurrection of the dead, and eternal judgment." These words do not refer to what the author is doing in his epistle (written around the same time as Paul's Pastoral Epistles). It is a reference to the "teaching" the recipients had already received years earlier—no doubt orally—from the founding teachers of the church. In fact, the author distances what he is doing in his letter from this earlier teaching, declaring that he has no intention of re-laying that foundation (5:12 and 6:1–2). He has other material he wants to give them (which, of course, builds on the original "teaching") because he wants them to "go on to maturity." At the end of the epistle, he describes his lengthy piece of communication not as "teaching" but as "a word of exhortation" (Heb. 13:22).

27. These words capture the thrust of his lectures, but the quotation comes from a booklet produced for Anglican ordinands: Donald Robinson, *Ordination for What?* (Sydney: Anglican Information Office, 1991), 19. I suggest that the former Archbishop of Sydney would agree with my extrapolation from what he said.

28. Donald Robinson, *Faith's Framework: The Structure of New Testament Theology* (Sutherland, NSW: Albatros, 1985), 141. Again, this statement represents the substance of what Robinson taught us in class.

29. Douglas J. Moo rejects a view similar to my own that he attributes to Walter Liefeld ("What Does it Mean Not to Teach or Have Authority over Men," in *Recovering Biblical Manhood and Womanhood* [ed. John Piper and Wayne Grudem; Wheaton, IL: Crossway, 2006], 181). Liefeld's argument is threefold: (1) Paul's ruling applied specifically to Ephesus, not to the universal church; (2) the passage is descriptive ("I do not permit") rather than prescriptive ("you should not permit"); (3) the verb *authenteō*, "to have authority," actually means *to take hold of authority*, not merely to *possess* it. See Walter Liefeld, "Women and the Nature of Ministry" (*JETS* 30 [1987]: 49–61). I do not agree with any of these points. In another article Liefeld suggests that "scholars should research whether teaching in the New Testament period had a dimension of authority that it no longer has, now that the Scriptures are so widely available and the doctrines of the church established" (Liefeld, "Response to David M. Scholer's 1 Timothy 2:9–15," 223). In a 2005 article Liefeld says, "Today the appropriate equivalent of these younger delegates representing the apostle Paul in the churches is not a local pastor but the canonical New Testament containing Paul's own words" (Walter Liefeld, "The Nature of Authority in the New Testament," in *Discovering Biblical Equality: Complementarity without*

*Hierarchy* [ed. R. W. Pierce, R. M. Groothuis, and G. D. Fee; Downers Grove, IL: InterVarsity Press, 2005], 262).

Similarly, New Testament scholar and friend Claire Smith has objected to using the production of the New Testament as a reason to silence a passage of the New Testament. "The Bible never hints," she remarks, "that the creation of a 'Bible' would render bits of 'the Bible' wrong or obsolete" (Claire Smith, *God's Good Design: What the Bible Really Says about Men and Women* [Sydney, Australia: Matthias Media, 2012], 49). I don't think of 1 Tim. 2:12 as "wrong" or "obsolete." I just think the teaching role Paul refers to in that passage has been transposed up a key or two because the "teachings" have been absorbed into the text of the New Testament. In any case, my central argument is not that, because we now have God's truth in writing, we no longer have to prevent women from expounding the truth in sermons. I am saying that 1 Tim. 2:12 never referred to "expounding the truth in sermons." It only ever meant preserving and laying down what the apostles had declared about the new covenant.

Claire Smith makes the additional point that we must not make too much of the distinction between the New Testament era and our own. After all, early churches had the Old Testament and some apostolic letters, and these letters were the "basis of ongoing instruction" (49). In chapter 2, I make clear just how few apostolic documents the churches in this period could have had access to: two or three pastoral letters from an apostle at most, and these letters represented only a tiny portion of what they already knew of the apostolic deposit. The difference between their era and ours is huge. More to the point, although I don't doubt that these apostolic letters became a focus for congregational study, reflection, and application, nowhere in the New Testament is such an exposition of these letters called "teaching." Claire Smith makes her underlying assumption plain when she says, "The teaching on view in this passage (as in the rest of the Pastoral Epistles) is the ongoing, authoritative and public exposition of God's truth (cf. 2:7; 4:11, 13, 16; 5:17; 6:2c–3). It is what we call 'the sermon,' the public authoritative proclamation of God's truth. The activity is what we call 'preaching'" (45). None of the passages referenced in this important statement, however, gives any indication that "teaching" is an "exposition" or a "sermon." That emerges as the "plain sense" reading only by assuming a definition of teaching derived from modern evangelical practice. Claire's published doctoral thesis, mentioned earlier, provides a more plausible account of *didaskein* or "teaching" (see especially chapter 3, "Core-teaching words")—and the words "sermon" or "exposition" are not mentioned. Claire Smith, *Pauline Communities*, 53-84.

30. You can hear examples a www.standrews.net.au.

31. There is an Old Testament passage that records an event involving something like exposition, though it is unlikely this text informed Paul's use of the term "teach." Ezra the priest calls the residents of Jerusalem together to hear the "Book of the Law of Moses that the Lord had commanded Israel" read out (in its entirety?) by Ezra himself (Neh. 8:1-3). Along the way, efforts are made by the Levites to ensure that the Israelites have understood the meaning—it has been a generation or more since the Law has been rehearsed before the nation:

> And Ezra the scribe stood on a wooden platform that they had made for the purpose. And beside him stood Mattithiah, Shema, Anaiah, Uriah, Hilkiah, and Maaseiah on his right hand, and Pedaiah, Mishael, Malchijah, Hashum, Hashbaddanah, Zechariah, and Meshullam on his left hand. And Ezra opened the book in the sight of all the people, for he was above all the people, and as he opened it all the people stood. And Ezra blessed the Lord, the great God, and all the people answered, "Amen, Amen," lifting up their hands. And they bowed their heads and worshiped the Lord with their faces to the ground. Also Jeshua, Bani, Sherebiah, Jamin, Akkub, Shabbethai, Hodiah, Maaseiah, Kelita, Azariah, Jozabad, Hanan, Pelaiah, the Levites, helped the people to understand the Law, while the people remained in their places. They read from the book, from the Law of God, clearly, and they gave the sense, so that the people understood the reading. (Neh. 8:4-8)

It is unclear whether the Levites are explaining the meaning of the language of this now-ancient Law or offering interpretative and practical insights about the text: "helping to understand" and "giving the sense" plausibly refers to either or both.

The Greek version of this passage, known as the Septuagint or LXX, offers different wording in the final lines, and Ezra himself is said to "teach" the people: "and they read the book of the law of God and Ezra taught [*didaskō*] and commanded in the knowledge of the Lord, and the people understood what was read." "Teach" here may mean simply that Ezra "laid down the law," so to speak. In that sense, it would be akin to the "teaching" of Moses and the priests of an earlier era when they rehearsed the words of the law for Israel (Lev 10:11; Deut. 4:1), or the "teaching" parents were to offer their children (Deut. 4:9), which involved reciting and mandating the words of Moses. Teaching in this sense is closer to the idea of repeating, reciting, or laying-down rather than explaining and applying. Alternatively, the Greek version of the Old Testament may mean that Ezra punctuated his reading of the Law with extemporary flourishes designed to clarify the meaning and press home the importance of what was being read. If this is the case, it offers a clear parallel to modern exposition. Whatever the meaning, the more obvious question is whether this particular Old Testament passage (in the Hebrew or the Greek) informs New Testament practice in any way and, more importantly, whether this is what Paul meant by "teaching." I think the answer is a clear "no" in both instances. Those who attempt to argue that *biblical exposition* is the New Testament definition of "teaching" usually assume what they are trying to prove.

32. "The vast majority of scholars assume that the Jewish Scriptures are in mind [in 2 Tim. 3:16]," notes Marshall, *The Pastoral Epistles*, 792. Note the context of 2 Tim.3:15, about the "sacred writings" that Timothy learned from his mother as a young boy.

33. There are two different understandings of this statement. (1) Paul means that the Old Testament itself—as Timothy reads it—teaches, reproves, corrects, and trains *him* as a ministry worker. (2) Paul means Timothy should read the Old Testament so that he might be able to teach, reprove, correct, and train *others*. If the former way of reading Paul's words is correct, "teaching" cannot refer to expounding the Bible. It refers, instead, to what the Scripture itself does when someone reads it (the same use of "teaching" appears in Rom. 15:4). With that said, I follow those commentators who think the second way of reading Paul's statement makes more sense in the context of 2 Tim. 3: he is saying that reading the Old Testament Scriptures will help his ministry to others. And it is on this interpretation that some might conclude that "teaching" refers to expounding the Scriptures.

34. Matthew occasionally speaks of Jesus "teaching *and preaching*" (Matt 4:23; 9:35; 11:1). These are obviously the same activity described from two perspectives. Jesus laid down his new covenant content, expecting listeners to receive and recall (and obey) his material. This is the central idea of "teaching," and Paul echoes it when he uses the word to refer to teachers laying down the deposit about Jesus first handed over by the apostles. "Preaching" (*kēryssō*), by contrast, has the sense of disclosing something new to the

public: it is an announcement. The content of Jesus' teaching—and frequently Paul's—was news to those who first heard it, so it could be described as teaching and preaching at the same time. This does not mean that these two words are precise synonyms, only that they overlap in content. Ulrich Luz in his excursus on "Preaching, Teaching, and the Gospel in Matthew" rightly notes, on the one hand, that "the addressees of *keryssein* are for [Matthew] the people of Israel and the Gentiles, never the disciples" and, on the other, that "the two terms [teaching and preaching] have different connotations, but in Matthew the substance is the same," namely, the gospel of the kingdom (Ulrich Luz, *Matthew 1-7* [Hermeneia; Philadelphia: Fortress, 2007], 168–69).

35. Marshall, *The Pastoral Epistles,* 381. So too Philip H. Towner, *The Goal of Our Instruction,* 121–29, 215. Mounce, *Pastoral Epistles,* 125–26, agrees that "teaching" is principally the authorized transmission of the apostolic doctrine of the Christian gospel.

36. Klaus Wegenast, "Teach," in *The New International Dictionary of New Testament Theology* (ed. Colin Brown; Grand Rapids: Zondervan, 1992), 3:765.

37. Smith, *Pauline Communties,* 56.

38. Claire has in her sights New Testament specialists such as James Dunn (*Jesus and the Spirit* [Philadelphia: Westminster, 1975], 347–50), who correctly stresses that "teaching" in the Pastorals is concerned with passing on the fixed deposit of apostolic material but exaggerates the free, charismatic experience of communication of the early Pauline letters. Dunn disputes that Paul was the author of the Pastoral Epistles.

39. There are some uses of "teaching" terminology in Paul that do not fit the pattern I have outlined. How relevant they are others can judge. For example, Paul mocks a Jewish teacher in Romans 2:17–21 in the words, "But if you call yourself a Jew and rely on the law and boast in God and know his will and approve what is excellent, because you are instructed from the law; and if you are sure that you yourself are a guide to the blind, a light to those who are in darkness, an instructor of the foolish, a *teacher* of children, having in the law the embodiment of knowledge and truth—you then who *teach* others, do you not *teach* yourself?" (italics added). Here, Paul is not talking about teaching in the approved, new covenant sense. He is challenging an imaginary Jewish instructor who sees his role as laying down for Gentiles the commandments of the Old Testament.

Romans 15:4 speaks about the Scriptures themselves (the Old Testament) being "written for our instruction [teaching; *didaskalia*]." But notice that Paul does not mean that the Old Testament was written so that we could teach the Old Testament. He is just saying that the Old Testament itself teaches us, presumably whenever it is read.

40. Moo, "What Does It Mean Not to Teach," 181.

41. Paul's explanation of his policy is notoriously difficult to interpret: "For Adam was formed first, then Eve. And Adam was not the one deceived; it was the woman who was deceived and became a sinner" (1 Tim. 2:13–14). For what it's worth, I think Paul's argument is as follows: Adam was formed first, according to the Genesis narrative, and so was the original custodian of the revelation of God ("You may surely eat of every tree in the garden, but of the tree of knowledge of good and evil you shall not eat," Gen. 2:16–17). The serpent saw a weak point in Eve and deceived her—something that Adam, as guardian of the commandment, should have protected her from. This matrix of ideas found expression in the church, says Paul, in the selection of certain *men* to guard the founding traditions of God's new revelation, so that the church might not be deceived. I cannot think that Paul is saying that women are more gullible than men. The apostle's high view of women in an ancient context is well documented: see, e.g., Thomas R. Schreiner, "The Valuable Ministries of Women in the Context of Male Leadership," in *Recovering Biblical Manhood and Womanhood* (ed. John Piper and Wayne Grudem; Wheaton, IL: Crossway, 2006), 211–27. (While I disagree with some of Schreiner's conclusions, particularly the claim that expository preaching is equivalent to ancient teaching, he does an excellent job of describing the many honours and roles Paul bestows on his female colleagues.) The principle Paul wishes to affirm is simply that of male headship or responsibility *for this particular discussion*, that is, for the teaching role. The reference to Eve's deception does not signal a theological principle—"women are easily fooled"—but a precedent or analogy. Grammatically, I see only the first clause ("For Adam was formed first") as offering the grounds of the ruling about male teaching. It is introduced by the causal conjunction *gar* ("because/for"). The second clause, however ("and Adam was not deceived, but the woman was deceived"), is introduced with *kai* ("and") and is, I think, a supplementary idea, as if Paul is simply adding, "And you remember how that particular story turned out!"

42. J. I. Packer, *The Proceedings of the Conference on Biblical Interpretation* (Nashville: Broadman, 1988), 114–15.

43. Doug Moo too quickly rejects the idea that the closing of the canon alters the nature of teaching: "The addition of an authoritative, written norm is unlikely to have significantly altered the nature of Christian teaching" ("What Does It Mean Not to Teach," 181). He offers his reasons in a single paragraph. First, he points out that Jewish teaching, which he thinks provided the historical model for Christian teaching, was heavily dependent on transmitting the Old Testament Scriptures, as well as the body of oral tradition. Therefore, Christian teachers will have inherited the pattern of scriptural exegesis as a core part of their role.

   I do not think this is accurate. If the Mishnah is anything to go by—and all would agree that this document is the clearest thing we have to a compendium of rabbinic teachings from the first and second centuries—exposition of the biblical text was *not* the typical form of Jewish teaching. The main concern of the Mishnah is to record the rulings of about 150 Jewish teachers on topics such as festivals, agriculture, legal damages, food laws, prayers, and so on. These are biblical topics, of course, and biblical quotations appear throughout, but exposition of Scripture hardly features. The central concern of the Mishnah is to record the *memorised sayings of the teachers*, which is why it was considered a "second Torah/Law," parallel to the written law of Moses. The New Testament's relationship to the Old Testament is strikingly similar to the Mishnah's relationship to the Old Testament (for Orthodox Jews). Rarely do New Testament writers "expound" passages of the Old Testament in anything like the modern sense. Instead, what we find are the remembrances and rulings of authoritative figures, whether apostles like John and Paul or transmitters of the apostolic traditions (i.e., "teachers") such as Mark, Luke, and the unknown author of Hebrews. It is all now received by the church as the Word of God, just as the Mishnah is regarded as "Torah" in Judaism.

   Second, Moo believes that the words of 2 Tim. 2:2 ("what you have heard from me in the presence of many witnesses entrust to faithful men who will be able to teach others also") suggest that authoritative teaching "would continue to be very important for the church." I do not doubt that Paul envisaged an important place for transmitters of the fixed oral traditions after his departure. Indeed, for several generations after Paul, the teacher *did* have a central place as a "walking reference library" of apostolic doctrine. But unless Paul was able to imagine a fixed New Testament canon, how could he *not* have envisaged an ongoing role for those who preserved the deposit of the faith? What Paul imagined to be the *form* of preservation and transmission of the apostolic deposit is not necessarily mandated for the church throughout time. To offer an analogy mentioned later in this book, Paul envisaged an ongoing "widows roll/roster" (1 Tim. 5:9–11). We happily admit that what Paul is really mandating here—the care of the needy—has morphed into the social services of the contemporary church. In a similar way, what Paul was mandating in 2 Tim. 2:2 was the careful transmission of the apostolic deposit itself, not the *form* that transmission would take into perpetuity. The teaching has been absorbed into the fixed New Testament. Whenever it is read, Paul's command to faithfully preserve the apostolic deposit is being fulfilled. I also think that some sermons do function as a deliberate mandating of apostolic material. The mission of 2 Tim. 2:2 continues on, but in a different key.

Finally, Moo concludes that "the Scriptures should be regarded as replacing the apostles, who wrote Scripture, not the teachers who exposited and applied it." This statement can be questioned from two angles. First, a significant part of the New Testament does not come from apostles at all, but from authoritative teachers of the apostolic tradition (Mark, Luke-Acts, Hebrews, James, Jude). It is not accurate to speak of a neat symmetry between the apostles and the New Testament (and then teachers and contemporary expositors). Second, there is a noticeable shift here in Moo's definition of the ancient teacher. He had previously defined authoritative teaching as the transmission of the apostolic deposit *and* the authoritative proclamation in light of that tradition. Now transmission fades from sight and exposition and application come to the fore. The shift makes ancient teachers sound like expositors. But this assumes what really needs to be demonstrated. I would not dispute that ancient teachers were involved in something like exposition (of the Old Testament as well as the memorised or written apostolic traditions). I can well imagine that their teaching—i.e., their transmission of the apostolic deposit—was frequently augmented with *explanations* and *exhortations* on the basis of the traditions. However, that should not distract us from observing that the constitutive purpose of teaching, as distinct from explanation, prophesying, exhorting, and preaching, was, as I hope I have demonstrated already, to pass on the memories, rulings, and insights of the apostles. Put another way, just because ancient "teaching" could combine with (or even morph into) "exhortation" does not mean that exhortation *is* teaching, any more than we would say that "exhorting" and "prophesying," which quoted the apostolic deposit, suddenly becomes "teaching." We have seen that Paul distinguishes between these two activities, and he only forbids one of them to women. In short, I think Moo's important paper too hastily dismisses the argument that since our only access to authoritative "teaching" is through the canon of Scripture, no one today performs a role exactly equivalent to that of the ancient teacher. Thus, it has to be asked whether Paul's prohibition against women "teaching" can legitimately be transposed to the biblical discourses we call "sermons." In any case, as I have said several times already, the key point is not that we do not have to prevent women from expounding God's truth now that we have the truth in written form. Rather, "teaching" in 1 Tim. 2:12 never referred to "expounding God's truth." It only ever meant preserving and laying down what the apostles had declared about the new covenant. Other New Testament words better describe our modern practice (exhorting, prophesying, preaching, etc.), none of which is restricted to men.

44. This is the context in which Paul says, "Women should keep silent in the churches. For they are not permitted to speak, but should be in submission, as the Law also says" (1 Cor. 14:34). All agree Paul cannot be contradicting what he said about women "praying or prophesying" in church just a few chapters earlier (11:5). So, "silence" here must mean nonparticipation in the activity he has just been describing: "the others [should] *weigh* what is said" (14:29, italics added). Given that "weighing" must mean checking the prophecies against the apostolic deposit or "teaching," I think Paul is simply saying that women, who may prophesy, are not to engage in the validation process. The meaning, then, is closely aligned to the injunction against women "teaching" in 1 Tim. 2:12. So also Carson, "Silent in the Churches," 133–47.

45. I agree with Carson that prophesying is "necessarily inferior in authority to the deposit of the truth" laid down by the apostles. Indeed, the former is to be weighed against the latter ("Silent in the Churches," 143). Where I would respectfully disagree with Carson is in the modern application of this ruling. I think the fixed canon of the New Testament, inasmuch as it is read and studied by the congregation, exercises a weighing function in all of church life. Contemporary sermons, just like ancient prophecy and exhortation, must be subject to this apostolic deposit.

46. Describing the ministry of an evangelist named Pantaenus, who preached in the mid-to-late second century, Eusebius in the fourth century writes,

"There *were up until then* a great many evangelists of the word" (Eusebius, *Ecclesiastical History* 5.10.2).

47. The full quotation from Calvin is fascinating: "'Evangelists' I take to be those who, although lower in rank than apostles, were next to them in office and functioned in their place. Such were Luke, Timothy, Titus, and others like them; perhaps also the seventy disciples, whom Christ appointed in the second place after the apostles (Luke 10:1). According to this interpretation (which seems to me to be in agreement with both the words and opinion of Paul), these three functions were not established in the church as permanent ones, but only for that time during which churches were to be erected where none existed before, or where they were to be carried over from Moses to Christ. Still, I don't deny that the Lord has sometimes at a later period raised up apostles, or at least evangelists in their place, as has happened in our own day. [Referring chiefly to Luther, whom he elsewhere often praises.] For there was need for such persons to lead the church back from the rebellion of Antichrist. Nonetheless, I call this office 'extraordinary,' because in duly constituted churches it has no place. Next come pastors and teachers, whom the church can never go without" (John Calvin, *Institutes of the Christian Religion* (ed. John T. McNeill; trans. Ford L. Battles; Philadelphia: Westminster, 1960), 2:1057.

48. You can find the primary sources for the early church widows roster/roll in Patricia Cox Miller, *Women in Early Christianity: Translations from Greek Texts* (Washington, DC: Catholic University of America Press, 2005), 49–61.

49. I can think of a couple of lines of research that might weaken my argument. First, it may be that a thorough investigation of all cognates of *didaskō/didachē* across the New Testament, not just in Paul, will find exceptions. I doubt any examples will be found where "teaching" means expounding and applying scriptural passages, but it is plausible that broader meanings can be found than the one I have insisted on for 1 Tim. 2:12 (laying down the apostolic deposit). However, whatever the results of such a study, I think I would still suggest that the Pauline usage should be our primary focus (rather than, say, how the Johannine writings employ the terminology), especially Paul's usage *in the Pastoral Epistles themselves* (since the prohibition against women teaching is found in one of those three letters.

A related argument that a friend offered begins with the observation that at the end of the first century a document was produced called the

*Didache* (*Teaching*). The content of that document goes far beyond any words we have from the apostles as recorded in the New Testament. So, is this a different use of the important term "teaching," one that weakens my case? I doubt it. Again, I would insist that Paul's usage should be the beginning and basis of our analysis of the meaning of the term in 1 Tim. 2:12. The naming of the *Didache* could only provide *secondary* evidence, since it comes from well outside Paul's circle. With that said, I suspect the *Didache* got its title precisely because the author(s) associated the Greek term *didachē* with the apostolic deposit. The full title is "The Teaching of the Lord for the Nations through the Twelve Apostles." The work purports to be a compendium of the material handed down by all the apostles and, as one recent study notes, probably "originated in the period when the gospel material still circulated orally" (Jonathan A. Draper, "The Didache," in *The Apostolic Fathers: An Introduction* [ed. Wilhelm Pratscher; Waco, TX: Baylor University Press, 2010], 9). This explains why the *Didache* was one of the few texts the early Christians thought *might* properly belong to the canon of the New Testament (but which they, thankfully, excluded because of doubts about its authorship). If anything, the naming of the *Didache* supports what I have been saying about the Pauline use of the term: teaching essentially means laying down what the apostles originally said about Jesus and the new covenant.

I have no doubt that within time the word "teaching" in the early church came to mean explaining and applying the written words of the New Testament (and entire Bible). That would be an interesting line of research, but I am not sure it would overturn the evidence that in 1 Tim. 2:12 Paul had a different meaning of this important term.

50. Packer, *The Proceedings of the Conference on Biblical Interpretation*, 114-15.

*Here's another book by John Dickson*

# The Christ Files

## How Historians Know What They Know about Jesus

*John Dickson*

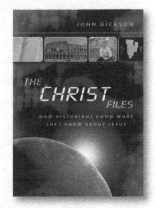

In *The Christ Files*, a four-session small group Bible study, scholar John Dickson examines the Christian faith through a historical look at the Christian faith and life of Jesus from both Scriptural and other non-Bible documentation.

Unique among the world's religions, the central claims of Christianity concern not just timeless spiritual truths, but tangible historical events as well. Historian John Dickson examines Christianity's claims in the light of history, opening you and your group to a wealth of ancient sources and explaining how mainstream scholars—whether or not they claim Christian Faith personally—reach their conclusions about history's most influential figure, Jesus of Nazareth.

In *The Christ Files*, Dickson skillfully highlights sources and historical methods used to study Christianity's assertions. He illustrates how historians assess the reliability of data, and provides an honest and informed perspective on where historical issues are clear-cut and where personal faith comes into play.

*The Christ Files* will help you and your small group expand your understanding of early Christianity and the life of Jesus.

*Available in stores and online!*